Editor
Mary S. Jones, M.A.

Managing Editor
Karen J. Goldfluss, M.S. Ed.

Cover Artist
Brenda DiAntonis

Art Production Manager
Kevin Barnes

Art Coordinator
Renée Christine Yates

Imaging
Rosa C. See

Publisher

Mary D. Smith, M.S. Ed.

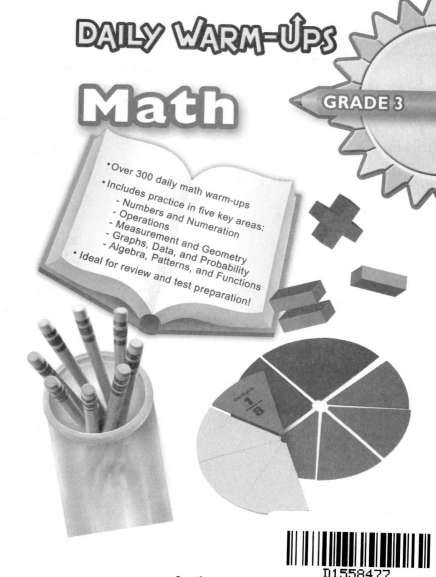

DAILY WARM-UPS
Math
GRADE 3

- Over 300 daily math warm-ups
- Includes practice in five key areas:
  - Numbers and Numeration
  - Operations
  - Measurement and Geometry
  - Graphs, Data, and Probability
  - Algebra, Patterns, and Functions
- Ideal for review and test preparation!

D1558477

Author

Heath Roddy

Teacher Created Resources, Inc.
6421 Industry Way
Westminster, CA 92683
www.teachercreated.com
ISBN 13: 978-1-4206-3961-2
© 2006 Teacher Created Resources, Inc.
Reprinted, 2010
Made in U.S.A.

The classroom teacher may reproduce copies of materials in this book for classroom use only. Reproduction of any part for an entire school or school system is strictly prohibited. No part of this publication may be transmitted, stored, or recorded in any form without written permission from the publisher.

Teacher Created Resources

Table of Contents

Table of Contents

Introduction

The *Daily Warm-Ups: Math* series was written to provide students with frequent opportunities to master and retain important math skills. The unique format used in this series provides students with the opportunity to improve their own fluency in math. Each section consists of at least 30 pages of challenging problems that meet national and state standards. (See Table of Contents to find a listing of specific subject areas. Answer keys are located at the back of each section.) Use the tracking sheet on page 6 to record which warm-up exercises you have given to your students. Or, distribute copies of the sheet for students to keep their own record.

This book is divided into five sections. The sections are as follows:

- Numbers and Numeration
- Operations
- Measurement and Geometry
- Graphs, Data and Probability
- Algebra, Patterns and Functions

Daily Warm-Ups: Math gives students a year-long collection of challenging problems to reinforce key math skills taught in the classroom. As students become active learners in discovering mathematical relationships, they acquire a necessary understanding that improves their problem-solving skills and, therefore, boosts their confidence in math. When using this book, keep the idea of incorporating the warm-ups with the actual curriculum that you may be currently using in your classroom. This provides students with a greater chance of mastering the math skills.

This book can be used in a variety of ways. However, the exercises in this book were designed to be used as warm-ups where students will have the opportunity to work problems and obtain immediate feedback from their teacher. To help ensure student success, spend a few moments each day discussing problems and solutions. This extra time will not take very long and will yield great results from students! As you use this book, you will be excited to watch your students discover how exciting math concepts can be!

Teaching Tips

Ideas on how to use the warm-ups are as follows:

- *Discussion*—Most warm-ups can be completed in a short amount of time. When time is up, model how to correctly work the problems. You may wish to have students correct their own work. Allow time for students to discuss problems and their solutions to problems. You may want to allow students the opportunity to discuss their answers or the way they solved the problems with partners. Discuss why some answers are correct and why others are not. Students should be able to support their choices. Having students understand that there are many ways of approaching a problem and strategies used in dealing with them are a great benefit for all students. The time you allow students to do this is just as important as the time spent completing the problems.

- *Review*—Give students the warm-up at the end of the lesson as a means of tying in an objective taught that day. The problems students encounter on each warm-up are designed to improve math fluency and are not intended to be included as a math grade. If the student has difficulty with an objective, review the material again with him or her independently and provide additional instruction.

 Introduction

Teaching Tips *(cont.)*

- *Assessment*—The warm-ups can be used as a preliminary assessment to find out what your students know. Use the assessment to tailor your lessons.
- *Introduction*—Use the warm-ups as an introduction into the new objective to be taught. Select warm-ups according to the specific skill or skills to be introduced. The warm-ups do not have to be distributed in any particular order.
- *Independent Work*—Photocopy the warm-up for students to work on independently.
- *Transparencies*—Make overhead transparencies for each lesson. Present each lesson as a means of introducing an objective not previously taught, or have students work off the transparency.
- *Model*—Invite students to come to the board to model how they approached a problem on the warm-up.
- *Test Preparation*—The warm-ups can be a great way to prepare for math tests in the classroom or for any standardized testing. You may wish to select warm-ups from all sections to use as practice tests and/or review prior to standardized testing.

Student Tips

Below is a chart that you may photocopy and cut out for each student. It will give students a variety of strategies to use when dealing with difficult problems.

 -

Math Tips

✓ Write word problems as number problems.

✓ Underline the question and circle any key words.

✓ Make educated guesses when you encounter multiple-choice problems or problems with which you are not familiar.

✓ Leave harder problems for last. Then, come back to solve those problems after you have completed all other problems on the warm-up.

✓ Use items or problem-solving strategies, such as drawing a diagram or making a table to solve the problem.

✓ Always check your answer to see that it makes sense.

Tracking Sheet

Numbers and Numeration Warm-Ups

1		8		15		22		29		36		43		50		57	
2		9		16		23		30		37		44		51		58	
3		10		17		24		31		38		45		52		59	
4		11		18		25		32		39		46		53		60	
5		12		19		26		33		40		47		54		61	
6		13		20		27		34		41		48		55		62	
7		14		21		28		35		42		49		56			

Operations Warm-Ups

1		8		15		22		29		36		43		50		57	
2		9		16		23		30		37		44		51		58	
3		10		17		24		31		38		45		52		59	
4		11		18		25		32		39		46		53		60	
5		12		19		26		33		40		47		54		61	
6		13		20		27		34		41		48		55		62	
7		14		21		28		35		42		49		56			

Measurement and Geometry Warm-Ups

1		8		15		22		29		36		43		50		57	
2		9		16		23		30		37		44		51		58	
3		10		17		24		31		38		45		52		59	
4		11		18		25		32		39		46		53		60	
5		12		19		26		33		40		47		54		61	
6		13		20		27		34		41		48		55		62	
7		14		21		28		35		42		49		56			

Graphs, Data and Probability Warm-Ups

1		8		15		22		29		36		43		50		57	
2		9		16		23		30		37		44		51		58	
3		10		17		24		31		38		45		52		59	
4		11		18		25		32		39		46		53		60	
5		12		19		26		33		40		47		54		61	
6		13		20		27		34		41		48		55		62	
7		14		21		28		35		42		49		56			

Algebra, Patterns and Functions Warm-Ups

1		8		15		22		29		36		43		50		57	
2		9		16		23		30		37		44		51		58	
3		10		17		24		31		38		45		52		59	
4		11		18		25		32		39		46		53		60	
5		12		19		26		33		40		47		54		61	
6		13		20		27		34		41		48		55		62	
7		14		21		28		35		42		49		56			

#3961 Daily Warm-Ups: Math   6   ©Teacher Created Resources, Inc.

NUMBERS AND NUMERATION

DAILY Warm-Up 1

Name _____ Date _____

1. Tyrone is counting the number of pennies he has saved. The table shows what he counted. How many pennies does Tyrone have? (*Circle the correct letter.*)

Hundreds	Tens	Ones
IIII	И II	И II

A. 499 **B.** 497 **C.** 487 **D.** 467

2. Which number below has a 4 in the thousands place and a 3 in the tens place? (*Circle the correct letter.*)

A. 3,431 **B.** 3,241 **C.** 4,235 **D.** 4,253

DAILY Warm-Up 2

Name _____ Date _____

1. Darrin has 5 black marbles and 3 white marbles. From the total of black and white marbles, which fraction below shows the number of black marbles Darrin has? (*Circle the correct letter.*)

A. $\frac{3}{3}$ **C.** $\frac{3}{8}$

B. $\frac{8}{3}$ **D.** $\frac{5}{8}$

2. Shade $\frac{3}{4}$ of the model below with your pencil.

Warm-Up 3

1. Lee bought a hamburger combo at Burger World. Lee paid for his lunch with a $5 bill. The cashier gave him back the money below. How much money did the cashier give him back? (*Circle the correct letter.*)

   A. $2.90

   B. $5.90

   C. $2.50

   D. $2.80

2. Look at the place value chart. Which answer choice identifies the chart correctly? (*Circle the correct letter.*)

   A. 50 + 4

   B. 500 + 4 + 2

   C. 500 + 40 + 2

   D. 54 + 2

Hundreds	Tens	Ones
5	4	2

Warm-Up 4

Name _____   Date _____

1. How many cubes does Jimmy have?

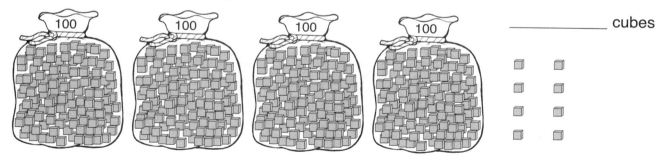

_____ cubes

2. Compare the two numbers below by writing the correct sign in the circle. Which place value tells you which number is greater?

456   459

Explain:_____

_____

_____

Name _____ **Date** _____

Warm-Up 5

1. Jane is writing a paper on presidents of the United States. When doing her research, she found the years that four presidents took office. Use the table below to show the order in which the presidents took office from the earliest to the most recent. (*Circle the correct letter.*)

   A. Washington, Johnson, Reagan, Carter

   B. Reagan, Carter, Johnson, Washington

   C. Washington, Reagan, Carter, Johnson

   D. Washington, Johnson, Carter, Reagan

Presidents in Office	
Jimmy Carter	1977
Lyndon Johnson	1963
George Washington	1789
Ronald Reagan	1981

2. Circle the letter that represents the number 39.

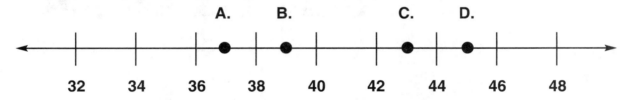

Name _____ **Date** _____

Warm-Up 6

1. Maci owns many shirts. More than $\frac{4}{8}$ of the shirts she owns have stripes. Which group could represent the shirts Maci owns? (*Circle the correct letter.*)

   A.

   B.

   C.

   D.

2. Which number has a 4 in the tens place and an 8 in the hundreds place? (*Circle the correct letter.*)

   A. 41,862 **B.** 12,840 **C.** 10,489 **D.** 29,428

Name _____ Date _____

1. Yesica earned the money below cleaning her grandmother's yard. How much money did Yesica earn? (*Circle the correct letter.*)

A. $4.00

B. $4.75

C. $4.85

D. $5.00

2. Shade in $\frac{3}{8}$ with your pencil.

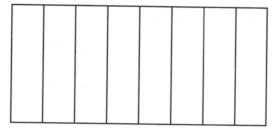

Name _____ Date _____

1. Which number is five hundred twelve? (*Circle the correct letter.*)

A. 5,012   B. 521   C. 512   D. 502

2. Which symbol will make this problem true? (*Circle the correct letter.*)

A. >

B. <

C. =

D. not given

934 943

Warm-Up 9

1. Write the sum for each problem.

   A. 5 tens + 6 ones = _____

   B. 9 tens + 5 ones = _____

   C. 6 tens + 2 ones = _____

   D. 4 tens + 9 ones = _____

2. The table shows the number of pages four friends read over the weekend. Which group shows the number of pages read in order from least to greatest? (*Circle the correct letter.*)

   A. Cody, Jane, Mark, Hank

   B. Hank, Mark, Cody, Jane

   C. Cody, Jane, Hank, Mark

   D. Hank, Mark, Jane, Cody

Friends	Jane	Mark	Hank	Cody
Pages Read	78	44	27	98

Warm-Up 10

1. Which number sentence is true? (*Circle the correct letter.*)

   A. 549 = five hundred fifty-nine

   B. 423 > four hundred thirty-three

   C. 289 < two hundred fifty-three

   D. 879 > eight hundred sixty-nine

2. Choose the fraction that represents the model below. (*Circle the correct letter.*)

   A. $\frac{2}{3}$ **C.** $\frac{2}{4}$

   B. $\frac{3}{4}$ **D.** $\frac{1}{3}$

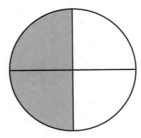

Name _____ **Date** _____

Warm-Up 11

1. Yolanda is the 12th person in line for tickets to a popular concert. There are 138 people in the line altogether. How many people are behind Yolanda? (*Show your work and write your final answer on the line.*)

_____ people

2. What is the value of the 4 in the number 3,456? (*Circle the correct letter.*)

   A. 4 thousands

   B. 4 tens

   C. 4 hundreds

   D. 4 ones

- -

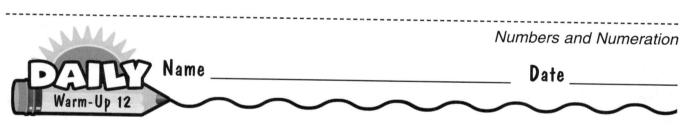

Name _____ **Date** _____

Warm-Up 12

1. Which number below has a 5 in the ten thousands place and an 8 in the tens place? (*Circle the correct letter.*)

   A. | 5 | 1 | 4 | 7 | 8 |

   B. | 8 | 2 | 7 | 7 | 0 |

   C. | 5 | 0 | 4 | 8 | 7 |

   D. | 5 | 5 | 4 | 7 | 8 |

2. Daveon wrote four numbers on separate sheets of paper. He arranged the numbers to make the smallest possible number using all four sheets of paper. What number did he make? (*Circle the correct letter.*)

   A. 9,842

   B. 2,489

   C. 9,428

   D. 2,948

| 9 | 8 | 2 | 4 |

Warm-Up 13

1. Which number below is between 5,429 and 7,567? (*Circle the correct letter.*)

    A. 5,419

    B. 5,426

    C. 6,293

    D. 7,593

5,429		7,567

2. Which of these best describes the numbers on the license plate? (*Circle the correct letter.*)

    A. They are all even numbers.

    B. They are all two-digit numbers.

    C. They are all odd numbers.

    D. They are all less than 9.

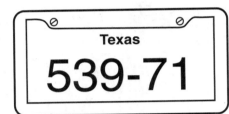

Texas

539-71

Warm-Up 14

1. Sam is counting the number of colored stickers he has. He found that $\frac{4}{5}$ of his stickers are gray. Which answer below correctly represents Sam's stickers? (*Circle the correct letter.*)

    A. ★★★★★★

    B. ★★☆☆☆

    C. ★★★★☆

    D. ★★★☆☆

2. How is the number 125,903 written in words? (*Circle the correct letter.*)

    A. Twelve thousand, nine hundred three

    B. One hundred twenty-five thousand, nine hundred three

    C. One thousand, nine hundred three

    D. One hundred twenty-five thousand, nine hundred thirty

DAILY Warm-Up 15

Name _____ Date _____

1. Write each number word in standard form.

A. ninety-seven   **B.** eighty-three   **C.** fifteen   **D.** one hundred

_____   _____   _____   _____

E. forty-nine   **F.** twenty-six   **G.** fifty   **H.** one hundred twelve

_____   _____   _____   _____

2. Write how many hundreds, tens, and ones are shown.

  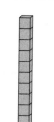

_____   _____   _____
hundreds   tens   ones

DAILY Warm-Up 16

Name _____ Date _____

1. Maci bought a group of balloons. Some of the balloons were white and the rest were gray. Write the fraction that shows the number of white balloons Maci bought.

2. Which fraction below has the most shaded? (*Circle the correct letter.*)

A. 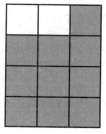   **B.** 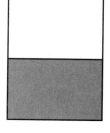   **C.** 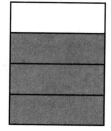   **D.**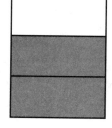

Name _____ **Date** _____

Warm-Up 17

1. Mrs. Harrison has reading stickers she gives her students. Some of the stickers are shaded and some are white. Mrs. Harrison only has 3 shaded stickers and 2 white stickers left. Which answer below represents this ratio? (*Circle the correct letter.*)

2. How is the number 98,428 written in words? (*Circle the correct letter.*)

   A. Ninety thousand, four hundred twenty-eight

   B. Nine hundred twenty-eight

   C. Ninety-eight thousand, four hundred twenty-eight

   D. Nine thousand, four hundred twenty-eight

Name _____ **Date** _____

Warm-Up 18

1. Gordon bought a bag of jawbreakers. He sorted the jawbreakers by color. The table shows the number of each color he has. Which fraction shows the number of jawbreakers that are blue? (*Circle the correct letter.*)

Color	Blue	Green	Red	Yellow
Number	3	2	4	2

   A. $\frac{2}{11}$ **B.** $\frac{3}{11}$ **C.** $\frac{2}{11}$ **D.** $\frac{4}{11}$

2. The table shows the number of miles four friends each drove over the weekend. Based on the table, which answer shows who drove the most miles from greatest to least? (*Circle the correct letter.*)

   A. Terry, James, Robin, Lee

   B. Lee, Robin, Terry, James

   C. Lee, Robin, James, Terry

   D. Terry, James, Lee, Robin

Person	Miles Driven
Terry	148
Lee	225
Robin	186
James	168

DAILY
Warm-Up 19

Name _____   Date _____

1. Which is true about the shaded numbers on the hundreds chart? (*Circle the correct letter.*)

   A. Numbers greater than 33 but less than 43 are shaded.

   B. Numbers greater than 42 but less than 53 are shaded.

   C. Numbers greater than 43 but less than 54 are shaded.

   D. Numbers greater than 42 but less than 54 are shaded.

1	2	3	4	5	6	7	8	9	10
11	12	13	14	15	16	17	18	19	20
21	22	23	24	25	26	27	28	29	30
31	32	33	34	35	36	37	38	39	40
41	42	43	44	45	46	47	48	49	50
51	52	53	54	55	56	57	58	59	60
61	62	63	64	65	66	67	68	69	70
71	72	73	74	75	76	77	78	79	80
81	82	83	84	85	86	87	88	89	90
91	92	93	94	95	96	97	98	99	100

2. Shade all even numbers on the hundreds chart that are greater than 63 but less than 72.

1	2	3	4	5	6	7	8	9	10
11	12	13	14	15	16	17	18	19	20
21	22	23	24	25	26	27	28	29	30
31	32	33	34	35	36	37	38	39	40
41	42	43	44	45	46	47	48	49	50
51	52	53	54	55	56	57	58	59	60
61	62	63	64	65	66	67	68	69	70
71	72	73	74	75	76	77	78	79	80
81	82	83	84	85	86	87	88	89	90
91	92	93	94	95	96	97	98	99	100

DAILY
Warm-Up 20

Name _____   Date _____

1. Romy is playing a game at the fair. If Romy shoots the basketball four times but doesn't earn the same score more than once, what is the highest score he could earn? (*Show your work and write your final answer on the line.*)

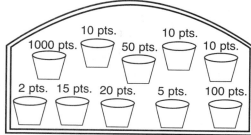

_____ points

2. The table shows the number of pages four friends each read over the week. Based on the table, which answer shows who read the most pages from least to greatest? (*Circle the correct letter.*)

   A. Sandy, James, Pete, Hank

   B. Hank, Pete, Sandy, James

   C. Hank, Pete, James, Sandy

   D. Sandy, James, Hank, Pete

Person	Pages Read
Sandy	147
Hank	225
Pete	186
James	168

DAILY Warm-Up 21

Name _____ **Date** _____

1. Follow the clues to answer the question.

- I am a two-digit number.
- I am not inside the rectangle.
- I am an odd number.
- I am inside the circle and pentagon.

89

72

45   44

34   61

What number am I? _____

2. Write each decimal in standard form. An example has been done for you.

Eight tenths = _____0.8_____

A. Four tenths = _____

B. Seven tenths = _____

C. Six tenths = _____

D. One and three tenths = _____

E. Two and four tenths = _____

F. Four and eight tenths = _____

G. Two and five tenths = _____

DAILY Warm-Up 22

Name _____ **Date** _____

1. Which number below has a 4 in the hundreds place and a 5 in the thousands place? (*Circle the correct letter.*)

A. 5 1 4 7 8   **C.** 5 0 4 8 7

B. 8 2 7 5 0   **D.** 8 5 4 7 8

2. Which point best represents $\frac{1}{4}$? (*Circle the correct letter.*)

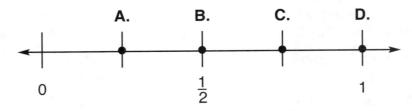

Name _____

Date _____

1. Jim counted 583 cars in a parking lot. Which answer shows the number of cars Jim counted? (*Circle the correct letter.*)

   A. five thousand, eighty-three

   C. five hundred eighty-three

   B. five hundred thirty-eight

   D. five hundred three

2. According to the table, how many points did the three friends earn altogether? (*Show your work and write your final answer on the line.*)

Friends	Sam	Pam	Pete
Points Earned	45	67	88

_____ points

- -

Name _____

Date _____

1. Michael read 29 pages last night. Travis read 62 more pages than Michael. How many total pages did Travis read? Show your work and write your final answer at the top of the grid. Then, shade the bubbles that match your answer.

⓪	⓪
①	①
②	②
③	③
④	④
⑤	⑤
⑥	⑥
⑦	⑦
⑧	⑧
⑨	⑨

2. Shade in the fractions below with your pencil. The first one has been done for you.

$\frac{1}{2}$ $\frac{3}{6}$ $\frac{6}{12}$

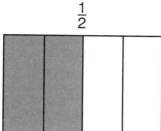

Name _____ **Date** _____

1. Write the value of the 8 in each number. An example has been done for you.

6,840 =	*800*

A. 68,950 _____

B. 6,078 _____

C. 8,562 _____

D. 7,286 _____

E. 83,250 _____

F. 8,912 _____

G. 28,102 _____

2. Complete the number sequences by choosing the correct number from the number bank that goes between each set of numbers.

A. 110 [ ] 132

B. 86 [ ] 98

C. 133 [ ] 145

D. 154 [ ] 160

E. 45 [ ] 77

F. 278 [ ] 301

G. 315 [ ] 330

H. 434 [ ] 474

Number Bank	
122	71
294	139
157	322
457	91

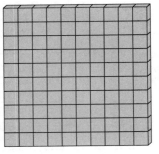

Name _____ **Date** _____

1. Circle two other ways to show 98.

8 tens and 9 ones   90 + 8   9 tens and 3 ones   9 tens and 8 ones

2. The model shows…

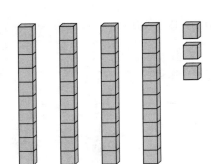

_____ hundred(s)

_____ ten(s)

_____ one(s)

Name _____ **Date** _____

Warm-Up 27

1. $\frac{1}{2}$ of 8 equals what number?

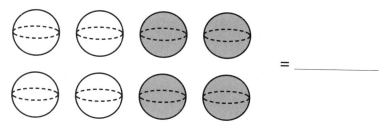

= _____

2. The model shows...

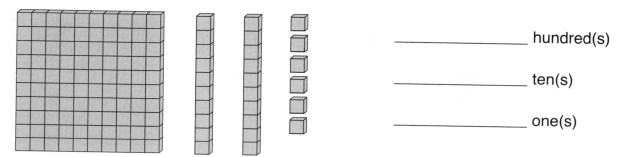

_____ hundred(s)

_____ ten(s)

_____ one(s)

- -

Name _____ **Date** _____

Warm-Up 28

1. Joan worked at her grandfather's apple farm over the summer. She picked 12,398 apples. Write the number of apples Joan picked in words on the line below.

_____

2. Choose a symbol from the box below to compare the two numbers.

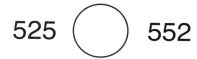

525 〇 552

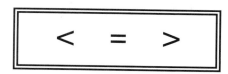

< = >

Name _____ Date _____

Warm-Up 29

Numbers and Numeration

1. Color $\frac{3}{9}$ of the pentagons below.

2. In words, write the number of points Sam and Pam scored altogether on the line below.

Friends	Sam	Pam	Pete
Points Earned	45	67	38

Sam and Pam scored _____ points.

Numbers and Numeration

Name _____ Date _____

Warm-Up 30

1. George has 1,632 acres of land. How is this number written in words? (*Circle the correct letter.*)

A. Six hundred thirty-two

C. One thousand, six hundred thirty-two

B. Six thousand, six hundred thirty-two

D. One thousand, six hundred twenty-three

2. Which problem below is true? (*Circle the correct letter.*)

A. 12,345 = one thousand, three hundred fifty-four

B. 23,981 = twenty-three thousand, nine hundred eighty-one

C. 20,319 = twenty thousand, three hundred nine

D. 15,209 = fifteen thousand, two hundred nineteen

DAILY Warm-Up 31

Name _____ Date _____

1. Which addition problem below has a sum of 284? (*Circle the correct letter.*)

   A. 2 hundreds + 5 tens + 6 ones = _____

   B. 2 hundreds + 8 tens + 4 ones = _____

   C. 2 hundreds + 4 tens + 8 ones = _____

   D. 2 hundreds + 9 tens + 8 ones = _____

2. Can you guess my number? Follow the clues.

   Clue 1 $12 \div 2 =$

   Clue 2 Take the quotient from the 1st clue and multiply it by 3.

   Clue 3 Take the product of clue 2 and add 5.

   Clue 4 Take the sum of clue 3 and subtract 6.

   What's my number? _____

DAILY Warm-Up 32

Name _____ Date _____

1. Which number sentence is false? (*Circle the correct letter.*)

   A. 18,549 = eighteen thousand, five hundred forty-nine

   B. 22,423 > twenty-two thousand, four hundred thirty-three

   C. 12,289 = twelve thousand, two hundred eighty-nine

   D. 22,879 > twenty-two thousand, eight hundred sixty-nine

2. Draw a circle. Divide the circle into 4 equal pieces. Using your pencil, shade in 2 pieces. What fraction of the circle is now shaded?

Name _____ **Date** _____

1. Which answer shows forty-three? *(Circle the correct letter.)*

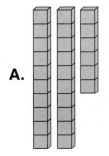 **A.** 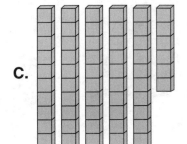 **B.** **C.** 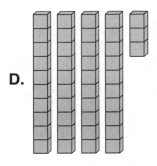 **D.**

2. Shade four of the rectangles with your pencil. What fraction of the whole rectangle is now shaded?

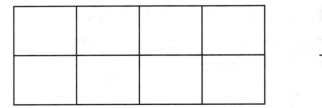

- -

Name _____ **Date** _____

1. Which numbers are missing from the number line?

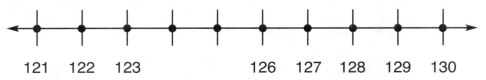

121 122 123   126 127 128 129 130

_____ and _____

2. Mr. Roberts works at a hardware store. The store was out of screwdrivers so he ordered some more. How many screwdrivers did Mr. Roberts order?

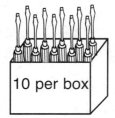 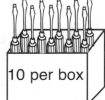 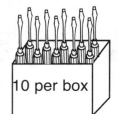 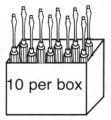 

_____ tens and _____ ones = _____ screwdrivers

Name _____ **Date** _____

1. Frankie saw birds sitting in 2 trees in his backyard. There were 36 birds in the first tree and 2 birds in the second tree. About how many birds did Frankie see altogether? (*Circle the correct letter.*)

   A. 60   **C.** 20

   B. 40   **D.** 30

2. Derrick has many locks. What fraction of Derrick's locks are open? (*Circle the correct letter.*)

   A. $\frac{3}{10}$ **B.** $\frac{7}{10}$ **C.** $\frac{3}{5}$ **D.** $\frac{2}{7}$

- -

Name _____ **Date** _____

1. What is the place value of the 4 in the number 24,693? (*Circle the correct letter.*)

   A. tens   **C.** thousands

   B. hundreds   **D.** ten thousands

2. What is the place value of each of the underlined numbers?

   A. 1̲2,985   **B.** 16̲,385   **C.** 54,3̲15   **D.** 32,5̲85

   _____   _____   _____   _____

DAILY Warm-Up 37

Name _____ Date _____

1. Write the value of each number on the place value chart. The first one is done for you.

	Ten Thousands	Thousands	Hundreds	Tens	Ones
2,345 =		2,000	300	40	5
18,312 =					
9,437 =					
37,658 =					

2. How do you know if a number is even or odd?

_____

_____

_____

_____

DAILY Warm-Up 38

Name _____ Date _____

1. Starting at the left, circle the thirteenth medal.

2. How many cubes are shown below?

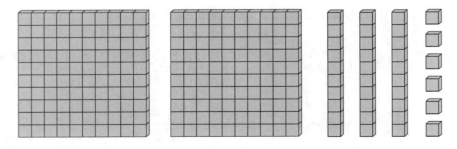

_____ hundreds _____ tens _____ ones = _____ cubes

Name _____ **Date** _____

1. What is the missing number on the number line? (*Circle the correct letter.*)

   A. 105

   B. 106

   C. 107

   D. 108

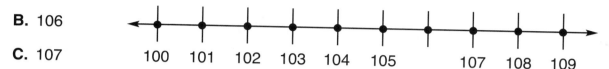

100 101 102 103 104 105   107 108 109

2. Brandi has a page of stickers. What fraction of the stickers are hexagons? (*Circle the correct letter.*)

   A. $\frac{9}{5}$ **B.** $\frac{5}{5}$ **C.** $\frac{5}{9}$ **D.** $\frac{2}{8}$

Name _____ **Date** _____

1. Write these numbers in order from least to greatest.

| 345 | 420 | 514 | 130 | 215 |

   _____ _____ _____ _____ _____

2. Solve the two problems below. Then, fill in the missing symbol in the circle to compare the answers.

   9 x 2 ◯ 20 – 4

   | < = > |

DAILY Warm-Up 41

Name _____ Date _____

1. Jake, Fred, Maria, and Joan each wrote the problems below. There is only one right answer. Which person wrote his or her problem correctly? (*Circle the correct letter.*)

   A. Jake

   B. Fred

   C. Maria

   D. Joan

Jake	163 < 136
Fred	136 = 112
Maria	197 < 210
Joan	78 < 62

2. What is the value of the 7 in the number 73,456? (*Circle the correct letter.*)

   A. 70,000   **B.** 7,000   **C.** 700   **D.** 70

DAILY Warm-Up 42

Name _____ Date _____

1. Which number below has a 5 in the tens place and an 8 in the ten thousands place? (*Circle the correct letter.*)

   A. | 5 | 1 | 4 | 5 | 8 |

   B. | 8 | 2 | 7 | 5 | 0 |

   C. | 5 | 0 | 4 | 8 | 7 |

   D. | 8 | 5 | 4 | 7 | 8 |

2. Wallace wrote the following numbers on cards. He arranged the cards to make the smallest number possible. What number did he make?

   3   9   2   4

   _____

Name _____ **Date** _____

Warm-Up 43

1. Write the numbers below in words.

A. 10,425 _____

B. 2,375 _____

C. 452 _____

D. 986 _____

2. Wanda made a lemon pie for her son. She cut it into 3 equal parts. Wanda ate $\frac{1}{3}$ of the pie. What fraction shows how much is left? Draw a picture to help you.

$$\frac{\boxed{}}{\boxed{}}$$

- -

Name _____ **Date** _____

Warm-Up 44

1. Look at the chart. Use your pencil to shade **even** numbers greater than 14 but less than 39.

1	2	3	4	5	6	7	8	9	10
11	12	13	14	15	16	17	18	19	20
21	22	23	24	25	26	27	28	29	30
31	32	33	34	35	36	37	38	39	40
41	42	43	44	45	46	47	48	49	50

2. Follow the directions below. Always begin counting from the left.

- Place an X inside the eighth triangle.
- Shade the fifth triangle.
- Circle the third triangle.

Name _____ **Date** _____

Warm-Up 45

1. Which answer choice below is true? (*Circle the correct letter.*)

   A. 23,419 = twenty thousand, nineteen

   B. 15,243 = fifteen thousand, two hundred three

   C. 18,710 = eighteen thousand, seven hundred ten

   D. 11,987 = eleven hundred seventy-eight

2. How many cubes are shown below?

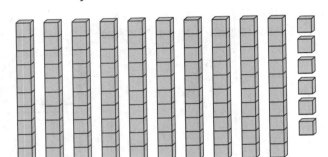

Hundreds	Tens	Ones

_____ cubes

Name _____ **Date** _____

Warm-Up 46

1. Jackie has a page of stickers. More than $\frac{6}{9}$ of the stickers are black. Which group could represent the page of stickers Jackie has? (*Circle the correct letter.*)

A.  **B.** **C.** 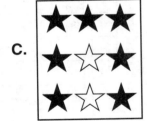 **D.**

2. Look at the hundreds chart. Use your pencil to shade **even** numbers greater than 43 but less than 60.

1	2	3	4	5	6	7	8	9	10
11	12	13	14	15	16	17	18	19	20
21	22	23	24	25	26	27	28	29	30
31	32	33	34	35	36	37	38	39	40
41	42	43	44	45	46	47	48	49	50
51	52	53	54	55	56	57	58	59	60
61	62	63	64	65	66	67	68	69	70
71	72	73	74	75	76	77	78	79	80
81	82	83	84	85	86	87	88	89	90
91	92	93	94	95	96	97	98	99	100

                                       ©*Teacher Created Resources, Inc.*

1. Cody and Gordon each wrote a fraction that identified this picture. What fractions could Cody and Gordon have written?

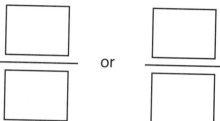 or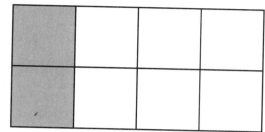

2. Which number is greater than 14,580? (*Circle the correct letter.*)

A. 14,581   **B.** 14,381   **C.** 14,579   **D.** 14,482

---

1. Which answer shows 26? (*Circle the correct letter.*)

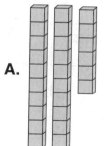 A.   B. 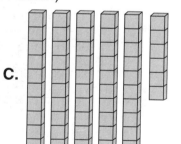 C. 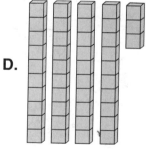 D.

2. Shade four of the rectangles with your pencil. What fraction of the whole rectangle is now shaded?

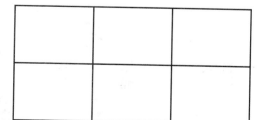 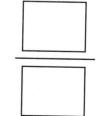

DAILY
Warm-Up 49

Name _____ Date _____

1. Look at the figures below. Which statement correctly describes the relationship between the two circles? (*Circle the correct letter.*)

A. $\frac{1}{2} = \frac{1}{2}$

B. $\frac{3}{4} > \frac{1}{2}$

C. $\frac{1}{4} > \frac{1}{2}$

D. $\frac{1}{2} > \frac{1}{4}$

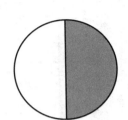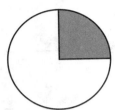

2. Look at the hexagons. What fraction of the hexagons are white? (*Circle the correct letter.*)

A. $\frac{8}{3}$ B. $\frac{8}{3}$ C. $\frac{5}{8}$ D. $\frac{8}{5}$

DAILY
Warm-Up 50

Name _____ Date _____

1. Look at the check below. Write the amount of the check next to where the arrow is pointing.

Name _____
Address _____
_____

$\frac{1\text{-}23}{789}$ No. _____

_____

Pay to the
Order of _____ $ |12,759|

_____ Dollars

BUFFALO BANK
321 Frontier Place
Prairie Grass, OK 82677

Memo _____   _____

2. Jason bought a new car for twenty-six thousand, five hundred eighty-three dollars. How is this number written in standard form? (*Circle the correct letter.*)

A. $20,583   B. $26,583   C. $23,538   D. $32,385

DAILY **Warm-Up 51**

Name _____ Date _____

1. The table below shows the number of members in a teaching organization from different cities. Which list shows the cities in order from the most members to the least members? (*Circle the correct letter.*)

   A. Houston, San Antonio, Dallas, Austin

   B. Austin, Dallas, San Antonio, Houston

   C. Houston, San Antonio, Austin, Dallas

   D. Austin, Houston, San Antonio, Dallas

Organization Members	
City	**Members**
Houston	2,235
Dallas	1,253
San Antonio	1,734
Austin	1,235

2. The figures below are shaded to show how many panes were broken out of a window at Grove Elementary. Which figure shows the greatest number of panes broken? (*Circle the correct letter.*)

   A. 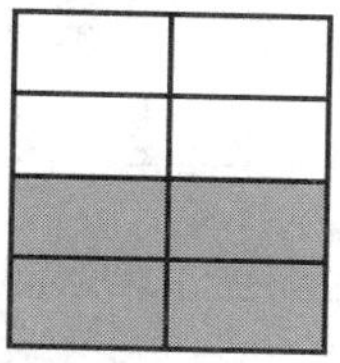   **B.** 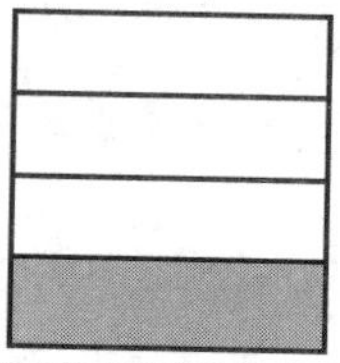   **C.** 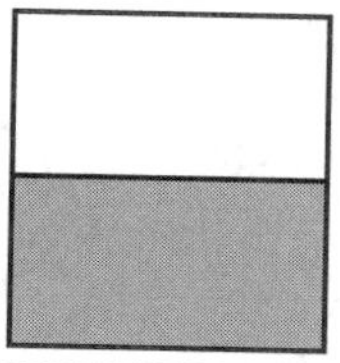   **D.**

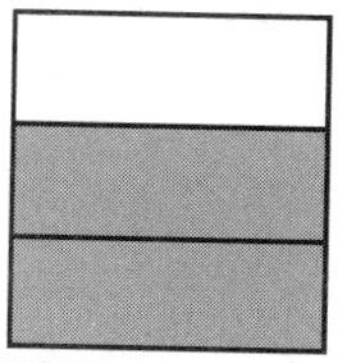

- -

DAILY **Warm-Up 52**

Name _____ Date _____

1. What is the value of 8 in the number 18,691? (*Circle the correct letter.*)

   A. 8,000   **B.** 80,000   **C.** 800,000   **D.** 8,000,000

2. Donna is doing an art project with her daughter. The table below shows the number of paper colors she has for the project. What fraction shows the number of sheets that are red? (*Circle the correct letter.*)

Color	Green	Blue	Red	White
Number	1	2	4	3

   A. $\frac{2}{10}$ **B.** $\frac{4}{10}$ **C.** $\frac{4}{8}$ **D.** $\frac{8}{10}$

Name _____ **Date** _____

1. Write the following numbers in standard form.

   A. Fifty-nine thousand, nine hundred ten   _____

   B. Forty-three thousand, six hundred twenty-three   _____

   C. Ninety-three thousand, five   _____

   D. Nine hundred sixty-one   _____

2. Write the place value of the 9 in each number.

   A. 96,341 _____ place   **E.** 1,596 _____ place

   B. 69,354 _____ place   **F.** 93,650 _____ place

   C. 4,679 _____ place   **G.** 6,912 _____ place

   D. 3,962 _____ place   **H.** 63,892 _____ place

- -

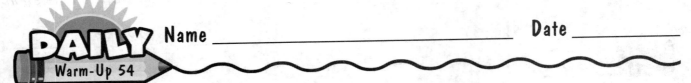

Name _____ **Date** _____

1. What is the place value of the 5 in the number 524,693? (*Circle the correct letter.*)

   A. hundreds   **C.** ten thousands

   B. thousands   **D.** hundred thousands

2. What is the place value of each of the underlined numbers?

   A. 9̲2,985   **B.** 66̲,385   **C.** 24,7̲15   **D.** 28,35̲7

   _____   _____   _____   _____

DAILY
Warm-Up 55

Name _____ Date _____

1. Write the value of each number on the place value chart. The first one is done for you.

	Ten Thousands	Thousands	Hundreds	Tens	Ones
9,535 =		9,000	500	30	5
58,312 =					
42,345 =					
17,067 =					

2. Janet bought a case of soda. The money below is what she received in change. How much money did Janet receive back? (*Circle the correct letter.*)

A. $4.56

B. $4.90

C. $5.10

D. $5.20

- -

DAILY
Warm-Up 56

Name _____ Date _____

1. Shade $\frac{5}{8}$ of the hexagons with your pencil.

2. The model shows…

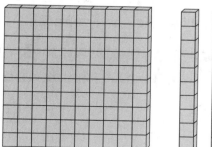   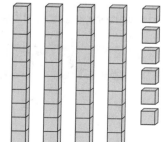

_____ hundred(s)

_____ ten(s)

_____ one(s)

DAILY **Warm-Up 57**

Name _____   Date _____

1. Round the following numbers.

To the nearest 100	
A. 149 _____	E. 518 _____
B. 294 _____	F. 157 _____
C. 825 _____	G. 182 _____
D. 211 _____	H. 762 _____

To the nearest 10	
I. 149 _____	M. 518 _____
J. 294 _____	N. 157 _____
K. 825 _____	O. 182 _____
L. 211 _____	P. 762 _____

2. Circle the largest number below.

12,310   12,942   12,430   12,899

DAILY **Warm-Up 58**

Name _____   Date _____

1. Six hundred fifty-seven people came to the fair on Friday. Two hundred twelve people came on Saturday. How many people went to the fair altogether? (*Show your work and write your final answer on the line.*)

_____ people

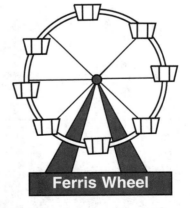

Ferris Wheel

2. Look at the place value chart. Which answer choice identifies the chart correctly? (*Circle the correct letter.*)

A. 7,000 + 300 + 9

B. 7,000 + 300 + 10 + 9

C. 700 + 30 + 1 + 9

D. 73 + 19

Thousands	Hundreds	Tens	Ones
7	3	1	9

DAILY Warm-Up 59

Name _____   Date _____

1. Which hundreds chart has even numbers greater than 58 but less than 89 shaded?
   (*Circle the correct letter.*)

A.

1	2	3	4	5	6	7	8	9	10
11	12	13	14	15	16	17	18	19	20
21	22	23	24	25	26	27	28	29	30
31	32	33	34	35	36	37	38	39	40
41	42	43	44	45	46	47	48	49	50
51	52	53	54	55	56	57	58	59	60
61	62	63	64	65	66	67	68	69	70
71	72	73	74	75	76	77	78	79	80
81	82	83	84	85	86	87	88	89	90
91	92	93	94	95	96	97	98	99	100

B.

1	2	3	4	5	6	7	8	9	10
11	12	13	14	15	16	17	18	19	20
21	22	23	24	25	26	27	28	29	30
31	32	33	34	35	36	37	38	39	40
41	42	43	44	45	46	47	48	49	50
51	52	53	54	55	56	57	58	59	60
61	62	63	64	65	66	67	68	69	70
71	72	73	74	75	76	77	78	79	80
81	82	83	84	85	86	87	88	89	90
91	92	93	94	95	96	97	98	99	100

2. Cody has some numbered balls. What fraction of the balls have a seven printed on
   them? (*Circle the correct letter.*)

   8   8   8   7   3   9   10   5   6   7

   A. $\frac{2}{10}$ **B.** $\frac{7}{10}$ **C.** $\frac{3}{5}$ **D.** $\frac{2}{7}$

DAILY Warm-Up 60

Name _____   Date _____

1. Dominic has these number cards on his desk. If he arranged the cards making the
   largest possible number, what number would Dominic make? (*Circle the correct letter.*)

   A. 975,421

   B. 957,421

   C. 924,571

   D. 924,517

   1   4   2   9   7   5

2. Janet is playing a game of darts. If she throws 3 darts and does
   not hit the same number twice, what is the highest possible score
   she could earn? (*Circle the correct letter.*)

   10
   20
   40
   50
   100

   A. one hundred sixty points

   B. one hundred seventy points

   C. one hundred eighty points

   D. one hundred ninety points

Name _____ **Date** _____

Warm-Up 61

1. At Lincoln Elementary, it is time for school pictures. Students are to line up from shortest to tallest. Frank is 54 inches tall, Janet is 43 inches tall, Linda is 39 inches tall, and Joe is 62 inches tall. In what order should these students line up for pictures?

_____, _____, _____, and _____

2. What is the value of the 7 in the number 73,456? (*Circle the correct letter.*)

   A. 70,000   **B.** 7,000   **C.** 700   **D.** 7

Name _____ **Date** _____

Warm-Up 62

1. Which number below has a 9 in the ten thousands place and an 8 in the tens place? (*Circle the correct letter.*)

   A. | 5 | 1 | 4 | 9 | 8 |

   B. | 9 | 2 | 7 | 9 | 0 |

   C. | 9 | 0 | 4 | 8 | 7 |

   D. | 6 | 5 | 4 | 8 | 1 |

2. Rico is fifth in line. Ernest is twelfth in the same line. Draw a picture showing Rico, Ernest, and everyone else.

Answer Key

Warm-Up 1
1. B
2. C

Warm-Up 2
1. D
2.

Warm-Up 3
1. D
2. C

Warm-Up 4
1. 408 cubes
2. < ; the ones place

Warm-Up 5
1. D
2. B

Warm-Up 6
1. C
2. B

Warm-Up 7
1. D
2.

Warm-Up 8
1. C
2. B

Warm-Up 9
1. A. 56
   B. 95
   C. 62
   D. 49
2. D

Warm-Up 10
1. D
2. C

Warm-Up 11
1. 126 people
2. C

Warm-Up 12
1. C
2. B

Warm-Up 13
1. C
2. C

Warm-Up 14
1. C
2. B

Warm-Up 15
1. A. 97
   B. 83
   C. 15
   D. 100
   E. 49
   F. 26
   G. 50
   H. 112
2. 2 hundreds, 1 ten, 2 ones

Warm-Up 16
1. $\frac{6}{12}$ or $\frac{1}{2}$
2. A

Warm-Up 17
1. A
2. C

Warm-Up 18
1. B
2. C

Warm-Up 19
1. D
2. 64, 66, 68, 70

Warm-Up 20
1. 1,170 points
2. A

Warm-Up 21
1. 61
2. A. 0.4
   B. 0.7
   C. 0.6
   D. 1.3
   E. 2.4
   F. 4.8
   G. 2.5

Warm-Up 22
1. D
2. A

Warm-Up 23
1. C
2. 200 points

Warm-Up 24
1. 91

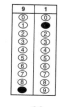

2. $\frac{3}{6}$ $\frac{6}{12}$

Warm-Up 25
1. A. 8,000
   B. 8
   C. 8,000
   D. 80
   E. 80,000
   F. 8,000
   G. 8,000
2. A. 122
   B. 91
   C. 139
   D. 157
   E. 71
   F. 294
   G. 322
   H. 457

Warm-Up 26
1. 90 + 8; 9 tens and 8 ones
2. 1 hundred, 4 tens, 3 ones

Warm-Up 27
1. 4
2. 1 hundred, 2 tens, 6 ones

Warm-Up 28
1. twelve thousand, three hundred ninety-eight
2. <

Warm-Up 29
1.
2. one hundred twelve

Warm-Up 30
1. C
2. B

Warm-Up 31
1. B
2. 17

Warm-Up 32
1. B
2. ; $\frac{2}{4}$ or $\frac{1}{2}$

Answer Key

Warm-Up 33
1. D
2. $\frac{4}{8}$ or $\frac{1}{2}$

Warm-Up 34
1. 124 and 125
2. 4 tens and 8 ones = 48 screwdrivers

Warm-Up 35
1. B   2. A

Warm-Up 36
1. C
2. A. ten thousands
   B. thousands
   C. hundreds
   D. tens

Warm-Up 37
1.

	Ten Thousands	Thousands	Hundreds	Tens	Ones
2,345 =		2,000	300	40	5
18,312 =	10,000	8,000	300	10	2
9,437 =		9,000	400	30	7
37,658 =	30,000	7,000	600	50	8

2. Answers will vary.

Warm-Up 38
1. Circle the 13th medal.
2. 2 hundreds, 3 tens, and 6 ones = 236 cubes

Warm-Up 39
1. B
2. C

Warm-Up 40
1. 130, 215, 345, 420, 514
2. >

Warm-Up 41
1. C
2. A

Warm-Up 42
1. B
2. 2,349

Warm-Up 43
1. A. ten thousand, four hundred twenty-five
   B. two thousand, three hundred seventy-five
   C. four hundred fifty-two
   D. nine hundred eighty-six
2. $\frac{2}{3}$; pictures will vary

Warm-Up 44
1. 16, 18, 20, 22, 24, 26, 28, 30, 32, 34, 36, 38 should be shaded
2.

Warm-Up 45
1. C
2. 0 hundreds, 10 tens, 6 ones = 106 cubes

Warm-Up 46
1. C
2. 44, 46, 48, 50, 52, 54, 56, 58 should be shaded

Warm-Up 47
1. $\frac{2}{8}$ or $\frac{1}{4}$
2. A

Warm-Up 48
1. A
2. $\frac{4}{6}$ or $\frac{2}{3}$

Warm-Up 49
1. D
2. C

Warm-Up 50
1. Twelve thousand, seven hundred fifty-nine
2. B

Warm-Up 51
1. A
2. D

Warm-Up 52
1. A
2. B

Warm-Up 53
1. A. 59,910
   B. 43,623
   C. 93,005
   D. 961
2. A. ten thousands
   B. thousands
   C. ones
   D. hundreds
   E. tens
   F. ten thousands
   G. hundreds
   H. tens

Warm-Up 54
1. D
2. A. ten thousands
   B. thousands
   C. hundreds
   D. tens

Warm-Up 55
1.

	Ten Thousands	Thousands	Hundreds	Tens	Ones
9,535 =		9,000	500	30	5
58,312 =	50,000	8,000	300	10	2
42,345 =	40,000	2,000	300	40	5
17,067 =	10,000	7,000	0	60	7

2. C

Warm-Up 56
1.
2. 1 hundred, 4 tens, 6 ones = 146

Warm-Up 57
1. A. 100   I. 150
   B. 300   J. 290
   C. 800   K. 830
   D. 200   L. 210
   E. 500   M. 520
   F. 200   N. 160
   G. 200   O. 180
   H. 800   P. 760
2. 12,942

Warm-Up 58
1. 869 people
2. B

Warm-Up 59
1. B
2. A

Warm-Up 60
1. A
2. D

Warm-Up 61
1. Linda, Janet, Frank, and Joe
2. A

Warm-Up 62
1. C
2. There should be a total of 12 people drawn. The 5th person in line should be labeled *Rico*. The 12th person in line should be labeled *Ernest*.

OPERATIONS

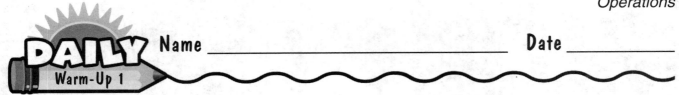

1. Mrs. Watkins has 12 flowers. She put an equal number of flowers in each of the 4 vases she owns. Which number sentence shows the number of flowers in each vase? (*Circle the correct letter.*)

A. $12 + 4 = 16$ **C.** $12 \times 4 = 48$

B. $12 - 4 = 8$ **D.** $12 \div 4 = 3$

2. Mrs. Mann and Mrs. Chilek each own large homes. There are 36 rooms in Mrs. Chilek's home and 18 rooms in Mrs. Mann's home. Estimate how many rooms are in both homes combined? (*Circle the correct letter.*)

A. 20   **B.** 50   **C.** 60   **D.** 70

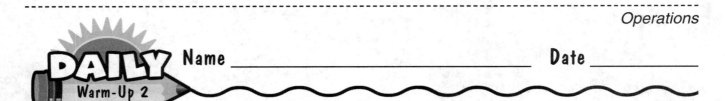

1. Isaac needed pencils for school. He bought 1 package of pencils that contained 8 green pencils, 4 yellow pencils, and 5 orange pencils. How many pencils does Isaac have? (*Show your work and write your final answer on the line.*)

_____ pencils

2. Jeffrey has 50 baseball cards. Damon has 20 more cards than Jeffrey. How can you find how many baseball cards Jeffrey and Damon have together?

You should _____

_____

_____

DAILY Warm-Up 3

Name _____ Date _____

1. Solve the problem.

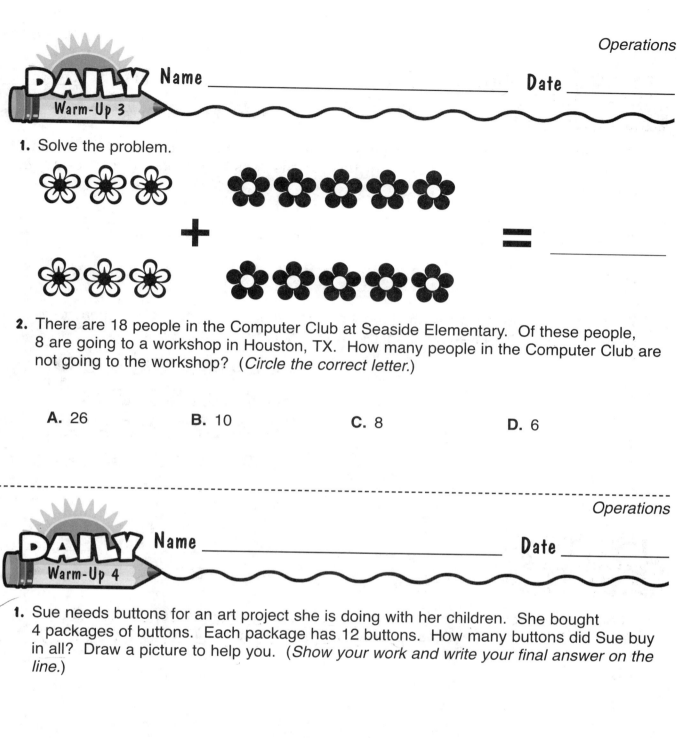

2. There are 18 people in the Computer Club at Seaside Elementary. Of these people, 8 are going to a workshop in Houston, TX. How many people in the Computer Club are not going to the workshop? (*Circle the correct letter.*)

A. 26   **B.** 10   **C.** 8   **D.** 6

- -

DAILY Warm-Up 4

Name _____ Date _____

1. Sue needs buttons for an art project she is doing with her children. She bought 4 packages of buttons. Each package has 12 buttons. How many buttons did Sue buy in all? Draw a picture to help you. (*Show your work and write your final answer on the line.*)

_____ buttons

2. Agnes bought 3 bags of tomatoes from the store. Each bag held 4 tomatoes. How many total tomatoes did Agnes buy? (*Show your work and write your final answer on the line.*)

_____ tomatoes

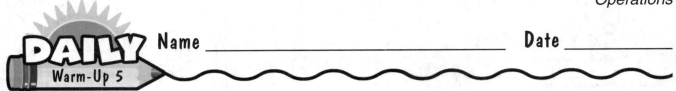

Name _____ Date _____

1. Ginger has 59 green hair ribbons and 82 yellow hair ribbons. She gave 27 yellow hair ribbons to her sister. About how many hair ribbons does Ginger now have? (*Circle the correct letter.*)

A. 60   **C.** 240

B. 110   **D.** 170

2. Betty placed 9 pictures on each of the 4 shelves in her living room. How many total pictures does Betty have on the shelves? (*Circle the correct letter.*)

A. 5   **C.** 36

B. 14   **D.** 45

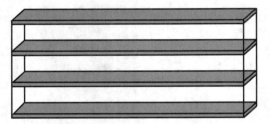

Name _____ Date _____

1. A school bus has 98 seats. Today, students are sitting in 56 seats. Which is the best estimate of the number of seats that are not being used? (*Circle the correct letter.*)

  A. 30   **C.** 140

  B. 40   **D.** 160

2. Jody bought a comic book for $2.50 and a hamburger combo for $4.99. If Jody used $10.00 to pay, which of these shows one way to find how much money Jody received back? (*Circle the correct letter.*)

  A. Add $2.50, $2.50, and $4.99.

  B. Add $2.50 and $10.00, then subtract the total from $4.99.

  C. Add $2.50 and $4.99, then add to $10.00.

  D. Add $2.50 and $4.99, then subtract the total from $10.00.

Name _____ **Date** _____

1. Jimmy bought 18 apples at the store. If he ate 3 apples each day, how many days will the apples last?

_____ days

2. Jerry spent $89 at the store. He spent $24 on a DVD movie and $44 on a new pair of shoes. The rest of the money was spent on school supplies. How much money did Jerry spend on school supplies?

Explain how you found the answer.

_____

_____ $ _____

_____

Name _____ **Date** _____

1. Clara has 150 dolls. She gave away $\frac{1}{3}$ of the dolls to her cousin. How many dolls does Clara have left? (*Show your work and write your final answer on the line.*)

_____ dolls

2. Six students showed up for the Computer Club party after school. Each student drank three cans of cola. How many cans of cola did they drink altogether? (*Circle the correct letter.*)

A. 9   **C.** 2

B. 3   **D.** 18

Name _____ **Date** _____

Warm-Up 9

1. Harry has 33 more toy cars than Hank. Which answer shows a possible number of toy cars Harry and Hank could have? (*Circle the correct letter.*)

   A. Harry 73 and Hank 45   **C.** Harry 110 and Hank 67

   C. Harry 74 and Hank 37   **D.** Harry 84 and Hank 51

2. Lorene went bowling with $20. After paying for the game and buying food, she had $8 left. If Lorene spent $7 on the game, how much money did she spend on food? (*Circle the correct letter.*)

   A. $5   **C.** $6

   B. $8   **D.** $9

- -

Name _____ **Date** _____

Warm-Up 10

1. Mrs. Erickson is having a meeting in her room with the parents of her students. She placed 8 large tables in her room with 6 chairs placed at each table. How many parents will have a place to sit? (*Circle the correct letter.*)

   A. 2   **C.** 36

   B. 14   **D.** 48

2. The local theater is putting on a play. On Friday, 456 people came to watch the play, and on Saturday, 389 people came to watch the play. What was the total number of people who came to watch the play on Friday and Saturday? (*Circle the correct letter.*)

   A. 755   **C.** 932

   B. 824   **D.** 845

DAILY Warm-Up 11

Name _____ Date _____

1. Roger went to a bookstore. He found 2 books he wanted to buy. The first book had 529 pages and the second book had 492 pages. How many more pages does the first book have than the second book? (*Circle the correct letter.*)

   A. 40   **C.** 41

   B. 35   **D.** 37

2. Lee needs to buy apples for the pies he is making. He finds bags of apples with 6 apples in each bag. If Lee bought 5 bags of apples, how many apples did he buy? Draw a picture to help you. (*Show your work and write your final answer on the line.*)

   _____ apples

DAILY Warm-Up 12

Name _____ Date _____

1. Sally and her family are going on vacation 564 miles away from home. The first day they drove 382 miles. How many more miles must they drive the second day to arrive at their vacation spot? (*Circle the correct letter.*)

   A. 946 miles   **C.** 182 miles

   B. 282 miles   **D.** 82 miles

2. Jerry picks oranges for a living. On Monday, he picked 452 oranges. On Tuesday, he picked 143 more oranges than he did on Monday. How many total oranges did Jerry pick on both days combined? (*Circle the correct letter.*)

   A. 2,135   **C.** 928

   B. 1,047   **D.** 1,135

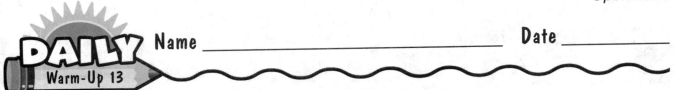

Name _____ **Date** _____

1. Peggy has a large fish tank. She bought 4 bags of fish with 3 fish in each bag. How many total fish did Peggy buy in all? Draw a picture to help you. (*Circle the correct letter.*)

A. 3

B. 7

C. 10

D. 12

2. George collects marbles. He plans to share 30 marbles with his cousins. If he wants to give 6 marbles to each cousin, how many cousins can George give marbles to? (*Show your work and write your final answer on the line.*)

_____ cousins

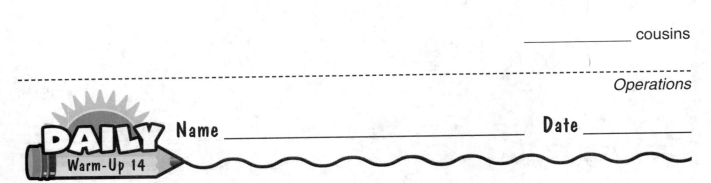

Name _____ **Date** _____

1. Solve the problems below.

A. $\begin{array}{r} 28 \\ -\ 7 \\ \hline \end{array}$ B. Eighteen – four = _____   C. $\begin{array}{r} 59 \\ -\ 3 \\ \hline \end{array}$

2. There are 24 students on the basketball team. Half of the students are taller than 6 feet. How many students on the team are taller than 6 feet?

How can you find the answer? _____

_____

_____   _____ students

Name _____ **Date** _____

Warm-Up 15

1. Jane collects teddy bears. She has 15 teddy bears in her collection. She wants to place an equal number of teddy bears on the shelves in her bedroom. If there are 3 shelves, how many teddy bears will she place on each shelf? (*Circle the correct letter.*)

   A. 15

   B. 3

   C. 18

   D. 5

2. Andrew has 18 letters that he wants to separate into 6 equal piles. How many piles will Andrew make if he does this correctly? (*Circle the correct letter.*)

   A. 3   **B.** 24   **C.** 4   **D.** 12

Name _____ **Date** _____

Warm-Up 16

1. When Mr. Lopez left his house, the temperature was 63° F. At noon, the temperature had gone up to 87° F. Which number sentence shows how to estimate the number of degrees the temperature had gone up? (*Circle the correct letter.*)

   A. 60° − 80° = ☐   **C.** 90° − 60° = ☐

   B. 80° − 60° = ☐   **D.** 60° + 90° = ☐

2. Marsha drove 105 miles today. Yesterday she drove 85 miles. How many more miles did Marsha drive today than yesterday? (*Show your work and write your final answer on the line.*)

   _____ more miles

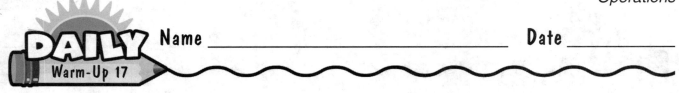

Name _____   Date _____

1. Ryan reads 25 pages each day. How many pages does Ryan read in one week?

Explain how to find the answer. _____

_____

_____

_____   _____ pages

2. Mrs. Harrison saw some horses in a field. There were 8 horses grazing, 3 horses standing, and 4 horses running. How many total horses did Mrs. Harrison see? (*Show your work and write your final answer on the line.*)

_____ horses

Name _____   Date _____

1. Mrs. Brooks raises hamsters. One cup of feed will last the hamsters four days. There are eight cups of feed left. How many days will the feed last? (*Show your work and write your final answer on the line.*)

_____ days

2. Mrs. Watkins tutors four boys after school a few times a week. She is paid $12.00 a day for each boy that she tutors. How much money will Mrs. Watkins earn each day tutoring? (*Circle the correct letter.*)

A. $24.00   **C.** $48.00

B. $36.00   **D.** $58.00

![DAILY Warm-Up 19] Name _____ Date _____

1. Sandra and her friends each sold 8 tickets to the school play. They sold a total of 40 tickets. Altogether, how many people sold the tickets? (*Circle the correct letter.*)

   A. 320   **C.** 32

   B. 48   **D.** 5

2. Jimmy has 56 cows. Nineteen of the cows are black. The rest of the cows are white and tan. How many cows are white and tan? (*Circle the correct letter.*)

   A. 43   **C.** 27

   B. 37   **D.** 75

![DAILY Warm-Up 20] Name _____ Date _____

1. Mr. Bren ordered 7 packages of markers for the new school year. There are 8 markers in each package. Circle the correct letter of the number sentence that shows how to find the total number of markers Mr. Bren ordered? Then, write the total in the box. Draw a picture to help you.

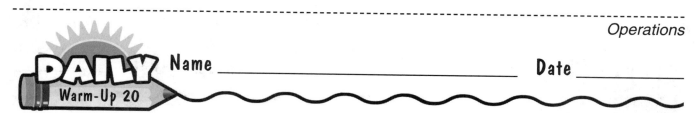

   A. $8 - 7 =$ [ ]   **B.** $7 \times 7 =$ [ ]   **C.** $8 \times 7 =$ [ ]   **D.** $8 + 7 =$ [ ]

2. Solve the subtraction problems below.

A. 94	B. 63	C. 99	D. 77	E. 74	F. 84
− 29	− 12	− 53	− 63	− 36	− 23

DAILY Warm-Up 21

Name _____ Date _____

1. Roy has 8 rabbits. What should he do to find the number of legs the 8 rabbits have altogether?

Explain: _____

_____

_____

_____

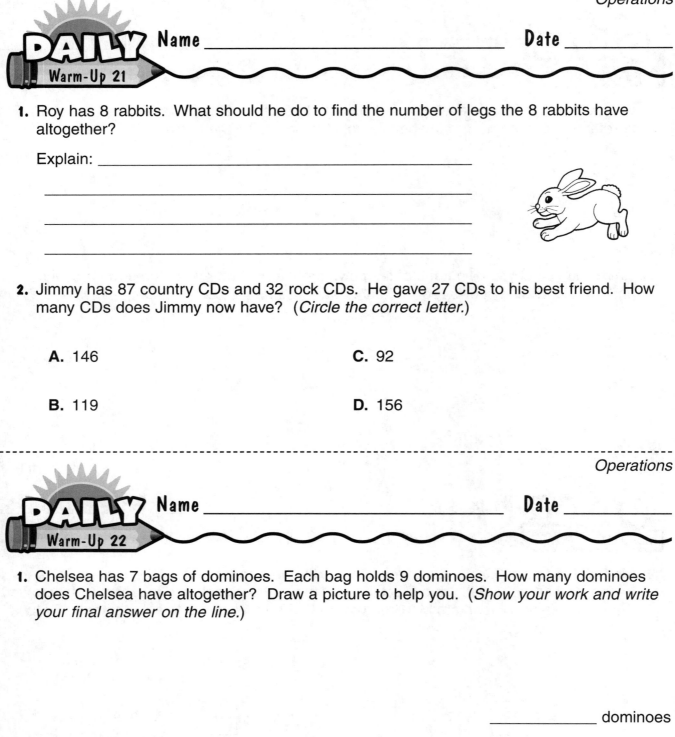

2. Jimmy has 87 country CDs and 32 rock CDs. He gave 27 CDs to his best friend. How many CDs does Jimmy now have? (*Circle the correct letter.*)

A. 146   **C.** 92

B. 119   **D.** 156

- -

DAILY Warm-Up 22

Name _____ Date _____

1. Chelsea has 7 bags of dominoes. Each bag holds 9 dominoes. How many dominoes does Chelsea have altogether? Draw a picture to help you. (*Show your work and write your final answer on the line.*)

_____ dominoes

2. Write a word problem for 20 ÷ 5 = 4.

_____

_____

_____

_____

_____

Name _____ **Date** _____

1. Eight students each bought a box of chocolate candy bars. There were 9 candy bars in each box. How many candy bars did they buy in all? (*Show your work and write your final answer on the line.*)

_____ candy bars

2. Solve the following problems.

A. 50	B. 182	C. 6	D. $15 \div 3 =$ _____
− 20	+ 47	x 4	

Name _____ **Date** _____

1. The table shows the number of soft drinks sold at a baseball game. Which number sentence can be used to find how many more grape sodas were sold than orange sodas? (*Circle the correct letter.*)

A. $784 - 463 =$ ☐

B. $784 + 567 =$ ☐

C. $784 - 567 =$ ☐

D. $784 + 463 =$ ☐

Drinks Sold	
Grape	784
Cola	1,974
Vanilla	463
Orange	567

2. Jerry is looking at two books to buy. The first book has 420 pages. The second book has 639 pages. How many more pages does the second book have than the first? (*Circle the correct letter.*)

A. 1,059   **B.** 959   **C.** 119   **D.** 219

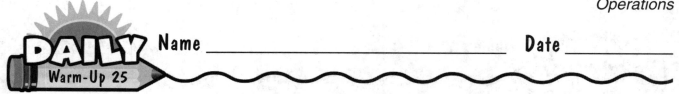

1. Jamison has 32 pictures that she wants to put on the shelves in her living room. There are 8 shelves. If she wants to put an equal number of pictures on each shelf, how many will go on each shelf? (*Show your work and write your final answer on the line.*)

_____ pictures

2. On Sue's farm, there are 143 chickens. On Heath's farm, there are 210 chickens. How could you find out how many more chickens Heath's farm has?

You should _____

_____

_____

- -

1. Jack is driving 452 miles to see his son graduate from college. He has already driven 198 miles. How many more miles does Jack still need to drive? (*Show your work and write your final answer on the line.*)

_____ more miles

2. Which answer is equal to 500 when rounded to the nearest hundred? (*Circle the correct letter.*)

    A. 410   **B.** 425   **C.** 445   **D.** 455

Warm-Up 27

1. Jan wants to give 4 cupcakes to each of her 3 children. How many cupcakes will Jan need?

Use addition to solve this problem.	Use multiplication to solve this problem.

2. Write a word problem for the number sentence 2 x 5 = 10.

_____

_____

_____

_____

Warm-Up 28

1. Beth canned 165 jars of jam over the summer. She had 58 jars of jam left over from last year. How many jars of jam does Beth have altogether? (*Show your work and write your final answer on the line.*)

_____ jars

2. Nancy babysat her niece for 3 hours. She earned $5.00 for each hour she worked. How much money was Nancy paid for babysitting? (*Circle the correct letter.*)

A. $12.00   **C.** $9.00

B. $10.00   **D.** $15.00

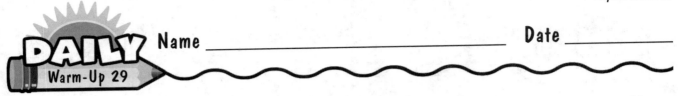

1. Mary has 189 chickens on her farm. She bought 243 chickens from her neighbor. How many chickens does Mary have in all? (*Show your work and write your final answer on the line.*)

_____ chickens

2. Ben has 15 trophies he wants to place on 3 shelves in his living room. If he placed an equal number of trophies on each shelf, how many trophies are on each shelf? (*Circle the correct letter.*)

A. 3   **C.** 18

B. 5   **D.** 45

1. Frank, Harry, George, and Mary sold raffle tickets. The table below shows the number of tickets sold by 3 of them. If all four students sold 198 tickets altogether, how many tickets did Mary sell? Show your work and write the answer in the table.

Raffle Tickets Sold	
Frank	33
Harry	54
George	63
Mary	

2. Tom ran 3 miles on Monday and 2 miles on Tuesday. On Wednesday, he ran twice as many miles as he did on Monday and Tuesday combined. How many miles did he run on Wednesday?

Explain: _____

_____

_____

_____ miles

Name _____ **Date** _____

Warm-Up 31

1. Julia baked 2 dozen cupcakes for her daughter's party at school. When the party was over, 6 cupcakes remained. How many cupcakes did the class eat? (*Show your work and write your final answer on the line.*)

_____ cupcakes

2. Robin has 89 quarters. Terry has 20 more quarters than Robin. How can you find the total number of quarters Robin and Terry have together?

You should_____

_____

_____

_____ _____ quarters

- -

Name _____ **Date** _____

Warm-Up 32

1. Jim has 21 ice cubes that he wants to put in 3 cups. He wants to put the same number of ice cubes in each cup. Which number sentence shows how many ice cubes Jim will put in each cup? (*Circle the correct letter.*)

A. 21 + 3 = 24

C. 21 − 3 = 18

B. 21 x 3 = 63

D. 21 ÷ 3 = 7

2. On Monday, Sandy worked 5 hours at her job. She earns $5 for each hour. If she works the same number of hours on Tuesday, how much money will Sandy have earned for the two days? (*Show your work and write your final answer on the line.*)

$ _____

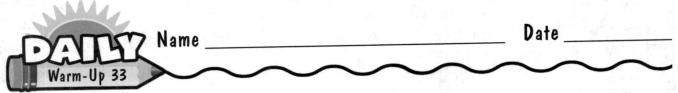

Name _____ **Date** _____

1. There are 24 students in Mrs. Clemen's morning class and 15 students in her afternoon class. When she ordered 1 pencil for each student, she rounded the number of total students to the nearest 10. Which number shows the best way to estimate the total pencils ordered? (*Circle the correct letter.*)

A. 50   **C.** 30

B. 20   **D.** 40

2. James is throwing a party. In his backyard, he places 9 large tables. At each table, he sets 8 chairs. When the party starts, how many people will have a place to sit? (*Circle the correct letter.*)

A. 71   **C.** 17

B. 45   **D.** 72

Name _____ **Date** _____

1. Terry finds many shells at the beach. She finds 8 large shells, 6 medium shells, and 7 small shells. If she places an equal number of shells into 3 containers, how many shells will go into each container? (*Show your work and write your final answer on the line.*)

_____ shells

2. Cody's car has 23,482 miles on it. Over the weekend, he drove another 234 miles. How many miles does Cody's car have on it now? (*Show your work and write your final answer on the line.*)

_____ miles

Name _____   **Date** _____

DAILY
Warm-Up 35

1. Wanda has some friends over for iced tea. She has 16 ice cubes. She places an equal number of ice cubes in each of the 4 glasses of tea she makes. Which number sentence shows the number of ice cubes she places in each glass? (*Circle the correct letter.*)

   A. 16 x 4 = 64   **C.** 16 ÷ 4 = 4

   B. 16 − 4 = 12   **D.** 16 + 4 = 20

2. Jennifer and Liz are participating in a 3-day walk-a-thon for cancer research. Each day, they will walk 20 miles. How many miles will Jennifer and Liz walk at the end of day three? (*Circle the correct letter.*)

   A. 30   **C.** 20

   B. 17   **D.** 60

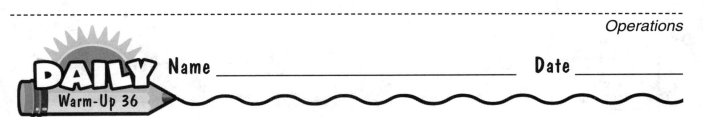

Name _____   **Date** _____

DAILY
Warm-Up 36

1. Terry is making tea for her husband and son. If 1 tea bag will make 2 cups of tea, how many tea bags will make 6 cups of tea? (*Show your work and write your final answer on the line.*)

_____ tea bags

2. Aaron has 3 notebooks. Each notebook will hold 80 sheets of paper. How many sheets of paper will the 3 notebooks hold altogether? (*Circle the correct letter.*)

   A. 277   **C.** 240

   B. 283   **D.** 280

DAILY
Warm-Up 37

Name _____ Date _____

1. Jimmy bought one dozen tamales. It costs $1.50 for six tamales. How much did Jimmy spend on tamales? (*Circle the correct letter.*)

A. $12.00   **C.** $1.50

B. $3.00   **D.** $18.00

2. Mrs. Rodriguez is a teacher. She grades 35 papers a day. How many papers does she grade in a typical school week of 5 days? (*Circle the correct letter.*)

A. 140   **C.** 35

B. 70   **D.** 175

DAILY
Warm-Up 38

Name _____ Date _____

1. Sam and Jack are blowing up balloons for Jack's birthday party. Jack blew up 6 balloons. Altogether, Sam and Jack blew up 15 balloons. How many balloons did Sam blow up? (*Circle the correct letter.*)

A. 9   **C.** 15

B. 8   **D.** 12

2. Jennifer's cat had 9 kittens. Three of the kittens were black and 2 were gray. The rest of the kittens were solid white. How many kittens were solid white? (*Circle the correct letter.*)

A. 2   **C.** 4

B. 3   **D.** 5

Name _____ **Date** _____

Warm-Up 39

1. There are 18 students in Mr. Wintzel's math class. Nine of the students are boys. How many of the students are girls? (*Circle the correct letter.*)

   A. 7   **B.** 11   **C.** 9   **D.** 8

2. Hank bought a puzzle for $1.50 and a new hat for $3.99. Which of these shows one way to find how much money Hank received back from $10.00? (*Circle the correct letter.*)

   A. Add $1.50, $1.50, and $3.99.

   B. Add $1.50 and $10.00, then subtract the total from $3.99.

   C. Add $1.50 and $3.99, then add to $10.00.

   D. Add $1.50 and $3.99, then subtract from $10.00.

Name _____ **Date** _____

Warm-Up 40

1. There are 93 seats on an airplane but only 52 passengers. Which expression shows how to find how many seats are not being used? (*Circle the correct letter.*)

   A. $93 \div 52 =$ ☐   **C.** $93 + 52 =$ ☐

   B. $93 - 52 =$ ☐   **D.** $93 \times 52 =$ ☐

2. Solve the problems below.

   A.   97
         + 34
         ‾‾‾‾

   B. $93 - 7 =$ _____

   C.   74
         − 8
         ‾‾‾‾

   D. $32 - 6 =$ _____

Name _____ **Date** _____

Warm-Up 41

1. Jane bought 2 dozen cupcakes for her daughter's class party. When the party was over, there were only 3 cupcakes left. Each student ate only 1 cupcake. Which expression shows how many students are in the class? (*Circle the correct letter.*)

   A. 12 + 12 = [ ]   **C.** 24 + 3 = [ ]

   B. 12 – 3 = [ ]   **D.** 24 – 3 = [ ]

2. Cindy counted the number of birds in a tree. Then, 18 birds flew away. Now there are only 23 birds left. How many birds did Cindy count to begin with? Explain.

   How can this problem be solved? _____

   _____

   _____   _____ birds

   _____

Name _____ **Date** _____

Warm-Up 42

1. Colin has 2 apple trees in his backyard. He counted 74 apples on the first tree. On the second tree, he counted 58 apples. How many apples are on both trees altogether? (*Show your work and write your final answer on the line.*)

   _____ apples

2. Solve each subtraction problem. Use the key to match the letter with the correct answer.

   1. 56 – 3 = [ ]

   2. 42 – 13 = [ ]

   3. 52 – 4 = [ ]

Key	
A	29
B	53
C	48

Name _____ **Date** _____

1. Jane had 3 quarters, 2 dimes, and 4 pennies. She spent 30 cents. How much money does Jane have left?

Explain: _____

_____

_____ _____ cents

_____

2. Last Friday night, the Giraffes and the Zebras had their championship basketball game. Based on the scoreboard, who won the game and how many points did they win by?

The _____ won by

_____ points.

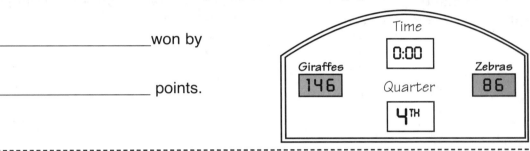

- -

Name _____ **Date** _____

1. One calculator reads the number 883. The other reads 235. What is the difference between the two numbers? (*Show your work and write your final answer on the line.*)

 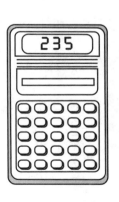

_____

2. Solve the problems below.

A. 85 + 17 = _____

B.   76
       + 35
      _____

C.   92
       − 23
      _____

DAILY
Warm-Up 45

Name _____ Date _____

1. Sue is making a dress. She has 12 each of green, yellow, orange, and red buttons. If she used all the green and red buttons, how many buttons did she use? (*Show your work and write your final answer on the line.*)

_____ buttons

2. Nancy has 16 cookies. She would like to give them to her friends so that each person has the same amount. If she has 4 friends, how many cookies can she give each friend? (*Show your work and write your final answer on the line.*)

_____ cookies

- -

DAILY
Warm-Up 46

Name _____ Date _____

1. Which number sentence below represents the picture? (*Circle the correct letter.*)

A. $10 - 5 = 6$

B. $10 + 5 = 15$

C. $10 \div 5 = 2$

D. $10 \times 5 = 50$

2. Each of the 22 students in Mrs. Watkins' class read 4 pages last night. How many total pages did they read altogether? (*Circle the correct letter.*)

A. 18

C. 46

B. 78

D. 88

DAILY Warm-Up 47

Name _____ Date _____

1. Travis needs 50 paintbrushes for an art class he teaches after work. He has 32 paintbrushes already. How many more must he get to have enough? (*Circle the correct letter.*)

   A. 22

   B. 82

   C. 18

   D. 38

2. Fernando has a page of star stickers. Which number sentence could be used to find how many of the star stickers are shaded? (*Circle the correct letter.*)

   A. 2 + 4 = ☐

   B. 2 + 3 = ☐

   C. 2 x 3 = ☐

   D. 2 x 4 = ☐

- -

DAILY Warm-Up 48

Name _____ Date _____

1. Look at the chart. Can you find the connecting squares with the numbers that add up to 18? Circle them. (*Hint:* The numbers can be connected vertically, horizontally, or diagonally. More than two numbers can be added together to make 18. There are 6 correct answers.)

13	6	9	8	0
8	5	11	5	9
14	8	1	12	7
12	5	9	2	2
7	10	5	4	3

2. There are 40 passengers on a bus that has no empty seats. Five passengers are sitting in each row. How many rows of seats are completely full of passengers?

   Explain: _____

   _____

   _____

   _____

   _____ rows

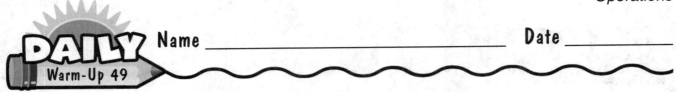

Name _____ **Date** _____

Warm-Up 49

1. Jared had 54 marbles. He lost 18 over the summer. How many marbles does Jared now have? (*Show your work and write your final answer on the line.*)

_____ marbles

2. Mrs. Hinojosa has fifty-three rose bushes in her garden. She planted twelve more over the holidays. How many rose bushes does Mrs. Hinojosa now have in her garden?

Explain: _____

_____

_____

_____ _____ rose bushes

Name _____ **Date** _____

Warm-Up 50

1. Charles saw four green socks, five yellow socks, two blue socks, and six red socks under his bed. How many socks did Charles see in all? (*Circle the correct letter.*)

A. 16   **C.** 11

B. 9   **D.** 17

2. Timothy saw one hundred sixty-three geese swimming in a pond. Twenty-eight geese got scared and flew away. How many geese are left in the pond? (*Show your work and write your final answer on the line.*)

_____ geese

Name _____ **Date** _____

Warm-Up 51

1. Which number sentence below represents the total number of bikes in this picture? (*Circle the correct letter.*)

    A. $7 - 4 = 3$

    B. $7 \times 4 = 28$

    C. $7 + 4 = 11$

    D. $28 \div 4 = 7$

2. Each child in the Computer Club sold 8 tickets for the laptop raffle. If there are 65 children in the Computer Club, how many tickets have been sold altogether? (*Show your work and write your final answer on the line.*)

_____ tickets

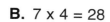

Name _____ **Date** _____

Warm-Up 52

1. Mrs. Robins is making sandwiches for her children's lunch. She has 6 children. She is putting 2 sandwiches in each child's lunch box. How many sandwiches does Mrs. Robins need to make? (*Circle the correct letter.*)

    A. 6   **C.** 8

    B. 4   **D.** 12

2. During P.E., Coach Steve divided the students into 9 teams with 7 students on each team. How many students are in the P.E. class? (*Show your work and write your final answer on the line.*)

_____ students

Name _____ **Date** _____

1. Mary baked a dozen cookies. She and her sister will share the cookies equally. How many cookies will each girl get? (*Show your work and write your final answer on the line.*)

_____ cookies

2. Janet has 24 dolls. Each doll has 3 dresses. How many doll dresses does Janet have altogether? (*Circle the correct letter.*)

A. 48   **C.** 76

B. 72   **D.** 27

- -

Name _____ **Date** _____

1. Dominic invited 12 friends to his birthday party. He wants to give each friend 2 party gifts. Which number sentence shows the number of party gifts Dominic needs? (*Circle the correct letter.*)

A. 12 + 2 = 14   **C.** 12 x 2 = 24

B. 12 − 2 = 10   **D.** 12 ÷ 2 = 6

2. David and Kerry are fence builders. David built 47 fences the first month and Kerry built 21 fences the second month. Estimate the number of fences David and Kerry built altogether? (*Show your work and write your final answer on the line.*)

_____ fences

Name _____ **Date** _____

Warm-Up 55

1. Janet walked 6 miles on Monday, 4 miles on Tuesday, 5 miles on Wednesday, and 7 miles on Thursday. If her goal is to walk 25 miles by Saturday, how many more miles must Janet walk on Friday to meet her goal? (*Show your work and write your final answer on the line.*)

_____ more miles

2. Use the key to find the numbers that make the problems true. (*Note:* Each number can only be used once.)

_____ x _____ = 21

_____ x _____ = 16

_____ x _____ = 30

Key		
3	2	5
6	7	8

- -

Name _____ **Date** _____

Warm-Up 56

1. Henry has 24 baseball cards. On his birthday, he received 6 more. How many baseball cards does Henry have now? (*Show your work and write your final answer on the line.*)

_____ baseball cards

2. Solve the problems below.

A.   62
     34
   + 57
   _____

B. $16 \div 4 =$ ☐

C.   905
   − 573
   _____

DAILY **Warm-Up 57**

Name _____ Date _____

1. Jeffrey has 157 marbles in the first jar and 59 marbles in the second jar. How many more marbles does Jeffrey have in the first jar than the second? (*Show your work and write your final answer on the line.*)

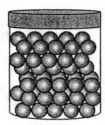 

_____ more marbles

2. Bobby wrote the problem 40 − 5 on a piece of paper. His sister worked the problem and gave the answer 35 back to Bobby. Which of the following could Bobby use to check his sister's answer to the problem? (*Circle the correct letter.*)

A. 35 x 5   **B.** 35 ÷ 5   **C.** 35 − 5   **D.** 35 + 5

DAILY **Warm-Up 58**

Name _____ Date _____

1. Terry is doing an art project with her niece. She bought 4 packages of glue sticks. There are 4 glue sticks in each package. How many glue sticks did Terry buy altogether? Draw a picture to help you. (*Show your work and write your final answer on the line.*)

_____ glue sticks

2. Solve the subtraction problems below.

A. 75
− 69

B. 93
− 57

C. 99
− 45

D. 78
− 35

E. 75
− 53

F. 74
− 54

Warm-Up 59

1. Coach Parson is rolling a cart with 12 basketballs into the gym for class. If he plans for 2 students to practice with 1 ball, and all of the basketballs on the cart are used, how many students are in Coach Parson's gym class? (*Circle the correct letter.*)

   A. 22

   B. 44

   C. 12

   D. 24

2. Coach Grant told each of her 22 students to do 8 push-ups during class. How many push-ups did the students do altogether? (*Circle the correct letter.*)

   A. 178   **B.** 168   **C.** 166   **D.** 176

Warm-Up 60

1. Solve the problems below.

   A. 83
         − 25
   _____

   B. 24 ÷ 3 =

   C. 9) 27

   D. 12
         x 7
         _____

2. Ricky eats 4 cookies after school each day. How many days will 24 cookies last? (*Show your work and write your final answer on the line.*)

_____ days

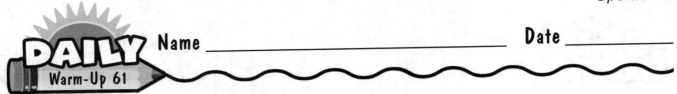

Name _____ **Date** _____

Warm-Up 61

1. Fill in the boxes with your own numbers. Then, add or subtract.

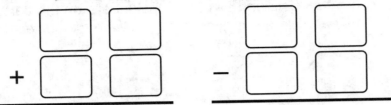

2. Jefferson saw 8 pigs at his uncle's farm. How many legs do 8 pigs have altogether?
(*Show your work and write your final answer on the line.*)

_____ legs

- -

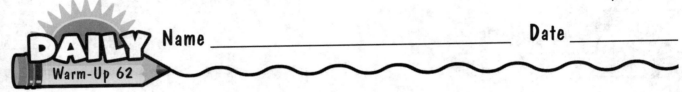

Name _____ **Date** _____

Warm-Up 62

1. Mandy is buying paintbrushes for her art class. She buys 5 packages of paintbrushes
with 4 paintbrushes in each package. How many total paintbrushes did Mandy buy?
Draw a picture to help you. (*Circle the correct letter.*)

A. 15

B. 9

C. 20

D. 24

2. Sarah bought 12 gifts. She gave an equal number of gifts to each of her 4 children.
Which number sentence shows the number of gifts each child was given? (*Circle the
correct letter.*)

A. 12 x 4 = 48

B. 12 ÷ 4 = 3

C. 12 − 4 = 8

D. 12 + 4 = 16

Answer Key

Warm-Up 1
1. D
2. C

Warm-Up 2
1. 17 pencils
2. You should add 50 to 20 to find Damon's total. Then add Damon's 70 cards to Jeffrey's 50 to get 120 baseball cards.

Warm-Up 3
1. 16
2. B

Warm-Up 4
1. 48 buttons
2. 12 tomatoes

Warm-Up 5
1. B
2. C

Warm-Up 6
1. B
2. D

Warm-Up 7
1. 6 days
2. You should add $24 and $44, then subtract that total from $89 to get $21.

Warm-Up 8
1. 100 dolls
2. D

Warm-Up 9
1. D
2. A

Warm-Up 10
1. D
2. D

Warm-Up 11
1. D
2. 30 apples

Warm-Up 12
1. C
2. B

Warm-Up 13
1. D
2. 5 cousins

Warm-Up 14
1. A. 21
   B. 14
   C. 56
2. 12 students; Divide 24 by 2

Warm-Up 15
1. D
2. A

Warm-Up 16
1. C
2. 20 more miles

Warm-Up 17
1. 175 pages; Multiply 25 and 7
2. 15 horses

Warm-Up 18
1. 32 days
2. C

Warm-Up 19
1. D
2. B

Warm-Up 20
1. C; 56
2. A. 65   D. 14
   B. 51   E. 38
   C. 46   F. 61

Warm-Up 21
1. Multiply 8 and 4 to get 32 legs.
2. C

Warm-Up 22
1. 63 dominoes
2. Answers will vary.

Warm-Up 23
1. 72 candy bars
2. A. 30
   B. 229
   C. 24
   D. 5

Warm-Up 24
1. C
2. D

Warm-Up 25
1. 4 pictures
2. You should subtract 143 from 210 to get 67 chickens.

Warm-Up 26
1. 254 miles
2. D

Warm-Up 27
1. Addition: 4 + 4 + 4 = 12 cupcakes
   Multiplication: 4 x 3 = 12 cupcakes
2. Answers will vary.

Warm-Up 28
1. 223 jars
2. D

Warm-Up 29
1. 432 chickens
2. B

Warm-Up 30
1. 48 tickets
2. 10 miles; Add 3 and 2 to get the combined total of 5 miles. Then double it to get 10 miles.

Warm-Up 31
1. 18 cupcakes
2. Add 20 and 89 to find the number of quarters Terry has. Then add Terry's 109 quarters to Robin's 89 quarters to get a total of 198 quarters.

Warm-Up 32
1. D
2. $50

Warm-Up 33
1. D
2. D

Warm-Up 34
1. 7 shells
2. 23,716 miles

Warm-Up 35
1. C
2. D

Warm-Up 36
1. 3 tea bags
2. C

Warm-Up 37
1. B
2. D

Warm-Up 38
1. A
2. C

Warm-Up 39
1. C
2. D

Warm-Up 40
1. B
2. A. 131
   B. 86
   C. 66
   D. 26

Warm-Up 41
1. D
2. Add 23 to 18 to get a total of 41 birds.

Warm-Up 42
1. 132 apples
2. 1. = B
   2. = A
   3. = C

Warm-Up 43
1. Subtract 30¢ from Jane's original 99¢ to get 69¢.
2. The Giraffes won by 60 points.

Warm-Up 44
1. 648
2. A. 102
   B. 111
   C. 69

Warm-Up 45
1. 24 buttons
2. 4 cookies

Warm-Up 46
1. D
2. D

Warm-Up 47
1. C
2. D

Warm-Up 48
1.

13	6	9	8	0
8	5	11	5	9
14	8	1	12	7
12	5	9	2	2
7	10	5	4	3

2. Divide 40 by 5 to get 8 rows.

Warm-Up 49
1. 36 marbles
2. Add 53 and 12 to get a total of 65 rose bushes.

Warm-Up 50
1. D
2. 135 geese

Warm-Up 51
1. B
2. 520 tickets

Warm-Up 52
1. D
2. 63 students

Warm-Up 53
1. 6 cookies
2. B

Warm-Up 54
1. C
2. 70 fences

Warm-Up 55
1. 3 more miles
2. 3 x 7 = 21 or 3 x 7 = 21
   8 x 2 = 16 or 2 x 8 = 16
   5 x 6 = 30 or 6 x 5 = 30

Warm-Up 56
1. 30 baseball cards
2. A. 153
   B. 4
   C. 332

Warm-Up 57
1. 98 more marbles
2. D

Warm-Up 58
1. 16 glue sticks
2. A.   6   D.   43
   B.   36   E.   22
   C.   54   F.   20

Warm-Up 59
1. D
2. D

Warm-Up 60
1. A. 58
   B. 8
   C. 3
   D. 84
2. 6 days

Warm-Up 61
1. Answers will vary.
2. 32 legs

Warm-Up 62
1. C
2. B

MEASUREMENT AND GEOMETRY

Daily Warm-Up 1

Name ______________________ **Date** __________

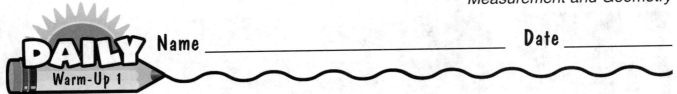

1. Which point best represents 150 on the number line? (*Circle the correct letter.*)

A. Point A

B. Point B

C. Point C

D. Point D

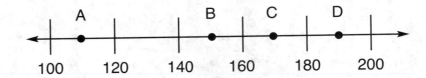

2. What shape is shown below? (*Circle the correct letter.*)

A. rectangle

B. circle

C. cube

D. square

Daily Warm-Up 2

Name ______________________ **Date** __________

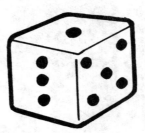

1. Beth loves drawing. Her drawing is shown below. What is the area of Beth's drawing? (*Circle the correct letter.*)

A. 24 square inches

B. 16 square inches

C. 26 square inches

D. 25 square inches

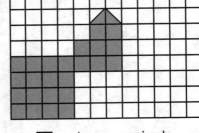

= 1 square inch

2. Jim placed an ad in the local newspaper for his lawn care business. Use your ruler to find the length of Jim's ad in centimeters. (*Circle the correct letter.*)

A. 12 cm

B. 10 cm

C. 8 cm

D. 6 cm

Jim's Lawn Care

Reasonable Prices

Call 979-543-LAWN

 ©Teacher Created Resources, Inc.

DAILY Warm-Up 3   Name _____   Date _____

1. Which shape below is a cylinder? (*Circle the correct letter.*)

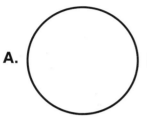 **A.**   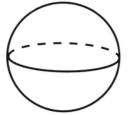 **B.**    **C.**   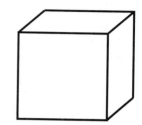 **D.**

2. Which unit would you use to measure the length of your classroom? (*Circle the correct letter.*)

   A. meter   **B.** millimeter   **C.** gram   **D.** liter

DAILY Warm-Up 4   Name _____   Date _____

1. Identify each shape below as either a plane shape (P) or solid shape (S). An example has been done for you.

   | ____P____ octagon | **C.** _____ hexagon |

   A. _____ cube   **D.** _____ pentagon

   B. _____ cylinder   **E.** _____ sphere

Key	
S	Solid Shape
P	Plane Shape

2. Which grid below has an area of 64 square inches? Note: ☐ = 1 square inch. (*Circle the correct letter.*)

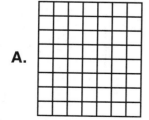 **A.**   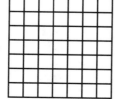 **B.**   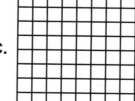 **C.**   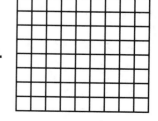 **D.**

Name _____ **Date** _____

1. Label the parts of the following shape.

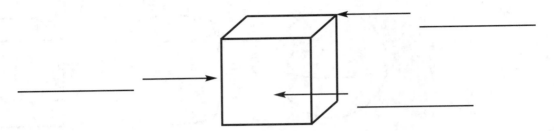

2. Connect the dots. What shape did you make? (*Circle the correct letter.*)

A. pentagon

B. hexagon

C. octagon

D. square

- -

Name _____ **Date** _____

1. How many quarts equal 1 gallon? (*Circle the correct letter.*)

A. 6   **C.** 4

B. 5   **D.** 3

2. Which figure is shown below? (*Circle the correct letter.*)

A. pentagon

B. hexagon

C. cube

D. cylinder

Name _____ **Date** _____

Warm-Up 7

1. Which puzzle pieces are congruent? (*Circle the correct letter.*)

A. 6 and 2   **C.** 5 and 4

B. 3 and 1   **D.** 3 and 6

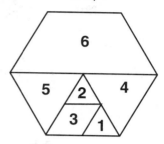

2. Look at the shapes. Which shape below does not belong? (*Circle the correct letter.*)

A.    **B.**    **C.** 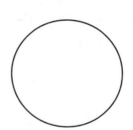   **D.**

- -

Name _____ **Date** _____

Warm-Up 8

1. Look at each figure below. Complete the table by writing the number of sides and the name for each shape.

	Number of Sides	Shape Name
A.		
B.		
C.		
D.		

2. Charles needs to be at work by 2:30. It takes him 15 minutes to get there. Which clock below shows the time Charles needs to leave home in order to be at work on time? (*Circle the correct letter.*)

A.    **B.**    **C.**    **D.**

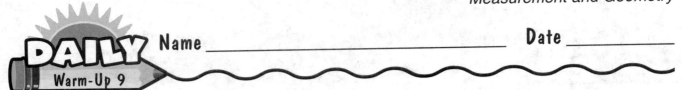

Name _____ **Date** _____

DAILY
Warm-Up 9

1. Fernando is weighing a book on a scale. Which choice below will balance the scale? Use the key below to help you find the answer. (*Circle the correct letter.*)

A.

B.

C.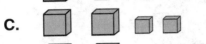

D.

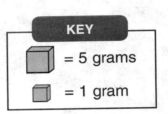

12 grams

2. Which shape does not belong? (*Circle the correct letter.*)

A.   **B.**   **C.**   **D.**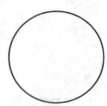

DAILY
Warm-Up 10

Name _____ **Date** _____

1. The Watkins family wants to change their backyard. The shaded part of the figure will be a walkway and the middle section is for a spa. What is the area of the shaded part of the backyard?

= 1 square foot

_____ square feet

2. Which figure does **not** show a line of symmetry? (*Circle the correct letter.*)

A. 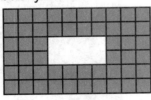   **B.** 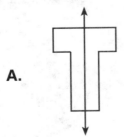   **C.** 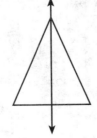   **D.**

DAILY **Warm-Up 11** Name _____ Date _____

1. Which pair of figures is congruent? (*Circle the correct letter.*)

A. 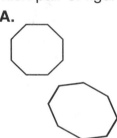 **B.** 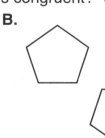 **C.**  **D.**

2. Which shape does not belong? (*Circle the correct letter.*)

A.  **B.**  **C.** 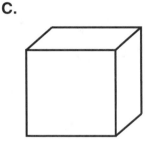 **D.**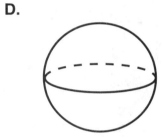

DAILY **Warm-Up 12** Name _____ Date _____

1. When Mr. Albert left his house this morning, the temperature was 30° F. Which thermometer shows this temperature correctly? (*Circle the correct letter.*)

A. 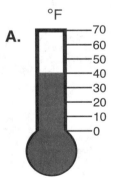 **B.** 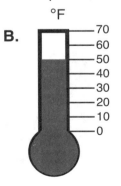 **C.** 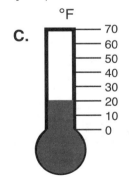 **D.**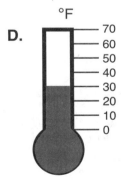

2. What measurement would be best to measure the length of your bedroom? (*Circle the correct letter.*)

A. inches   **B.** feet   **C.** millimeters   **D.** liters

Name _____ **Date** _____

DAILY
Warm-Up 13

1. Which shape could be made by the 2 triangles below? (*Circle the correct letter.*)

   A. pentagon

   B. cube

   C. rectangle

   D. hexagon

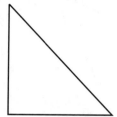 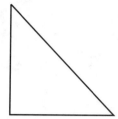

2. Are these two shapes congruent? Circle your answer and explain.

Explain:_____

_____

_____

_____

Yes or **No**

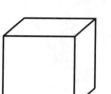 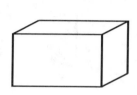

- -

Name _____ **Date** _____

DAILY
Warm-Up 14

1. The shape Jay drew on the chalkboard has 6 sides. Which shape below could Jay have drawn? (*Circle the correct letter.*)

    A. hexagon   **B.** pentagon   **C.** square   **D.** octagon

2. Fill in the blanks with the correct information.

   A.   **B.**   **C.**

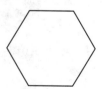

Number of sides _____   Number of sides _____   Number of sides _____

Name of shape _____   Name of shape _____   Name of shape _____

        82   ©*Teacher Created Resources, Inc.*

Name _____   **Date** _____

1. Which is a reasonable estimate of the distance between the top of a student's desk and the floor? (*Circle the correct letter.*)

A. 1 foot

B. 1 kilometer

C. 1 yard

D. 1 pound

2. Mike left for work at 7:45 A.M. He arrived at his job 45 minutes later. Mark the hands on the clock below to show the time Mike arrived at his job.

Left

Arrived

Name _____   **Date** _____

1. Sandra is making a garden that is 30 feet long and 10 feet wide. What is the perimeter in feet of Sandra's garden? Draw a picture to help you. (*Show your work and write your final answer on the line.*)

_____ feet

2. Use your ruler to measure the length of the pencil to the nearest inch. (*Circle the correct letter.*)

A. 6 inches   **B.** 7 inches   **C.** 8 inches   **D.** 9 inches

Name _____ **Date** _____

1. Which bear has a line of symmetry drawn correctly? (*Circle the correct letter.*)

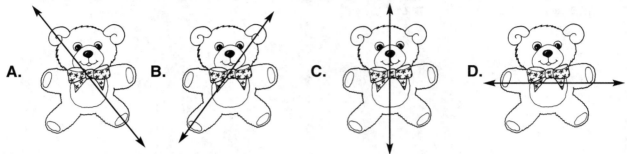

A.   **B.**   **C.**   **D.**

2. Congruent figures are the same size and same shape. Are the shapes below congruent?

Circle: **Yes** or **No**

Name _____ **Date** _____

1. Which describes the cube correctly? (*Circle the correct letter.*)

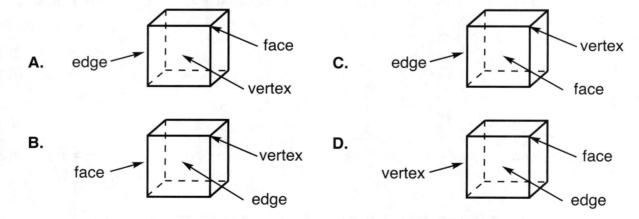

A. edge → face / vertex

C. edge → vertex / face

B. face → vertex / edge

D. vertex → face / edge

2. Which would be the best unit to measure the height of a door? (*Circle the correct letter.*)

A. liters   **B.** millimeters   **C.** centimeters   **D.** feet

DAILY
Warm-Up 19

Name _____ Date _____

1. Which shape below does **not** belong with the others? (*Circle the correct letter.*)

A.

B.

C.

D.

2. Which lines are **not** parallel lines? (*Circle the correct letter.*)

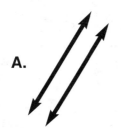

A.

B.

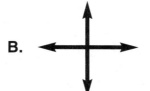

C.

D.

- -

DAILY
Warm-Up 20

Name _____ Date _____

1. Are the lines below parallel or perpendicular? How do you know?

_____

_____

_____

_____

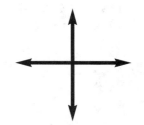

2. Jeff's birthday is September 28th. If today is September 3rd, how many days until Jeff's birthday?

_____ days

September						
SUNDAY	MONDAY	TUESDAY	WEDNESDAY	THURSDAY	FRIDAY	SATURDAY
					1	2
3	4	5	6	7	8	9
10	11	12	13	14	15	16
17	18	19	20	21	22	23
24	25	26	27	28	29	30

Name _____   **Date** _____

Warm-Up 21

1. Which would be the best unit to measure the weight of an elephant? (*Circle the correct letter.*)

   A. tons

   B. inches

   C. grams

   D. kilograms

2. In June, the Chess Club meets every Thursday. How many times will the Chess Club meet in June?

June						
SUNDAY	MONDAY	TUESDAY	WEDNESDAY	THURSDAY	FRIDAY	SATURDAY
					1	2
3	4	5	6	7	8	9
10	11	12	13	14	15	16
17	18	19	20	21	22	23
24	25	26	27	28	29	30

   The Chess Club will meet _____ times in June.

- -

Name _____   **Date** _____

Warm-Up 22

1. Jim drew the shapes below on the board. He challenged his friend to find which shape has less than 4 sides. If his friend answered correctly, which answer did he give? (*Circle the correct letter.*)

   A. W

   B. X

   C. Y

   D. Z

   W   **X**   **Y**   **Z**

2. James is putting in a new window in his house. What is the perimeter of the window James is installing? (*Circle the correct letter.*)

   A. 110 cm

   B. 120 cm

   C. 210 cm

   D. 220 cm

   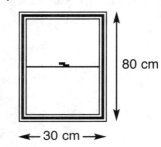

   80 cm

   ← 30 cm →

Name _____ **Date** _____

1. Which can be used to measure temperature? (*Circle the correct letter.*)

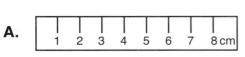

A.

B.

C.

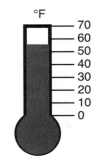

2. Look at the balance scale. How much does the camera weigh?

A. 300 grams

B. 200 grams

C. 250 grams

D. 650 grams

weighs 500 grams

weighs 100 grams

weighs 50 grams

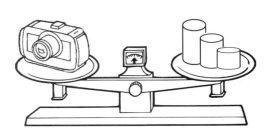

- -

Name _____ **Date** _____

1. Allen is making a patio in his backyard. The shaded part is the shape of the patio that Allen has designed. What is the area of Allen's patio?
(*Circle the correct letter.*)

A. 28 sq. ft.

B. 30 sq. ft.

C. 21 sq. ft.

D. 32 sq. ft.

▨ = 1 square foot

2. How many centimeters long is the marker?

_____ cm

cm 1 2 3 4 5 6 7 8 9 10 11 12

DAILY Warm-Up 25

Name _____   Date _____

1. Circle the heaviest object. (*Circle the correct letter.*)

A.   B.    C.    D.

2. Are the two shapes alike or different? Circle your answer.

Alike or **Different**

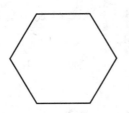 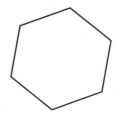

DAILY Warm-Up 26

Name _____   Date _____

1. Which point best represents 190 on the number line? (*Circle the correct letter.*)

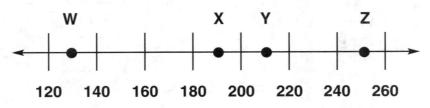

W   X   Y   Z

120   140   160   180   200   220   240   260

A. W   B. X   C. Y   D. Z

2. Use the calendar to answer the questions.

A. How many Mondays are in the month of June?

_____ Mondays

B. How many days are in the month of June?

_____ days

June						
SUNDAY	MONDAY	TUESDAY	WEDNESDAY	THURSDAY	FRIDAY	SATURDAY
					1	2
3	4	5	6	7	8	9
10	11	12	13	14	15	16
17	18	19	20	21	22	23
24	25	26	27	28	29	30

DAILY Warm-Up 27

Name _____ Date _____

1. Mary drew four shapes on the board. She asked her friend Sally to circle the shapes that are congruent. If Sally did this correctly, what two shapes did she circle?

 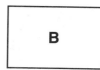

_____ and _____

2. Colin drove to his grandmother's house. He arrived 2 hours and 15 minutes later. Mark the hands on the clock below to indicate the time he arrived.

Left

Arrived

DAILY Warm-Up 28

Name _____ Date _____

1. Which is a set of parallel lines? (*Circle the correct letter.*)

A.   **B.**   **C.**   **D.**

2. Which object has the greatest weight? (*Circle the correct letter.*)

A. 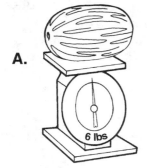   **B.**    **C.** 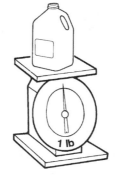   **D.**

Name _____ **Date** _____

Warm-Up 29

1. Which of the following could you use to find the weight of an object? (*Circle the correct letter.*)

     A. kilometers   **B.** liters   **C.** grams   **D.** meters

2. About how long would it take to run one mile? (*Circle the correct letter.*)

     A. 15 minutes   **B.** 45 minutes   **C.** 2 hours   **D.** 1 hour

- -

Name _____ **Date** _____

Warm-Up 30

1. Which shape has a line of symmetry drawn correctly? (*Circle the correct letter.*)

   A.   **B.**   **C.**   **D.**

2. Jennifer started mowing her lawn at 10:00 A.M. She finished 1 hour and 15 minutes later. Mark the time she finished mowing her lawn on the clock below.

DAILY Warm-Up 31 **Name** _____ **Date** _____

1. When Beth left her house, the temperature was 37°F. Three hours later, the temperature was 12 degrees warmer. Which thermometer shows the current temperature? (*Circle the correct letter.*)

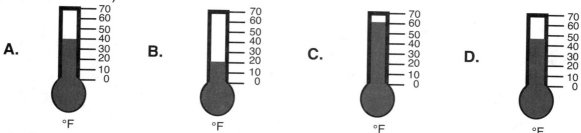

A. °F   B. °F   C. °F   D. °F

2. Look at each clock. Draw the hands of the clocks to indicate the correct times listed.

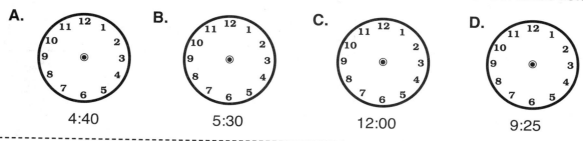

A. 4:40   B. 5:30   C. 12:00   D. 9:25

Measurement and Geometry Measurement and Geometry

DAILY Warm-Up 32 **Name** _____ **Date** _____

1. About how many centimeters long is the screwdriver?

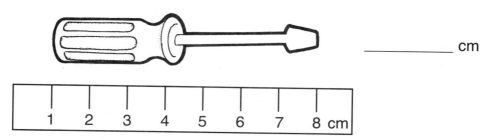

_____ cm

2. Which figure has a line of symmetry drawn correctly? (*Circle the correct letter.*)

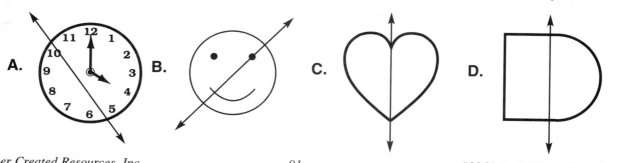

A.   B.   C.   D.

DAILY
Warm-Up 33

Name _____ Date _____

1. Name this figure. (*Circle the correct letter.*)

   A. cube

   B. rectangular prism

   C. cylinder

   D. sphere

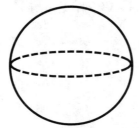

2. Which is **not** an example of a slide? (*Circle the correct letter.*)

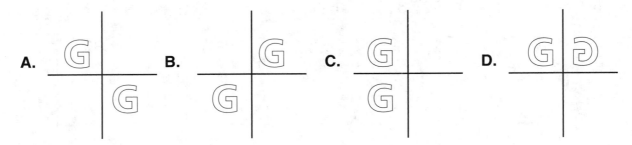

A.   B.   C.   D.

DAILY
Warm-Up 34

Name _____ Date _____

1. If there are 12 inches in 1 foot, how many inches are in 2 feet?

   There are _____ inches in 2 feet.

2. Jimmy bought 2 gallons of milk. How many quarts of milk does Jimmy have? (*Circle the correct letter.*)

   A. 2   **B.** 4   **C.** 8   **D.** 10

Name _____ **Date** _____

Warm-Up 35

1. How are these shapes different?

_____
_____
_____
_____
_____
_____

2. Draw and label a set of parallel lines and a set of perpendicular lines below.

Name _____ **Date** _____

Warm-Up 36

1. Which is true about the shape? (*Circle the correct letter.*)

A. It has 1 curved surface and 2 flat surfaces.

B. It has 1 curved surface and 3 flat surfaces.

C. It has 1 curved surface and 1 flat surface.

D. It has 3 curved surfaces and 3 flat surfaces.

2. Jeanne arrived home at 9:40 P.M. Which clock shows the time Jeanne arrived home? (*Circle the correct letter.*)

   A.   **B.**   **C.**   **D.**

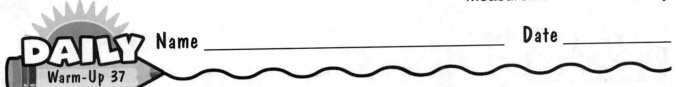

Name _____ **Date** _____

Warm-Up 37

1. Which is true about a triangular prism? Use the picture to help you. (*Circle the correct letter.*)

   A. A triangular prism has 2 faces.

   B. A triangular prism has 3 faces.

   C. A triangular prism has 4 faces.

   D. A triangular prism has 5 faces.

   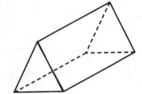

2. Which of these solid figures has eight vertices? (*Circle the correct letter.*)

 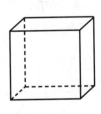  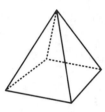

   A.   **B.**   **C.**   **D.**

Name _____ **Date** _____

Warm-Up 38

1. Janie wants to know how much water her bathtub will hold. Which is the best estimate of the capacity of a bathtub? (*Circle the correct letter.*)

   A. 30 meters   **B.** 30 gallons   **C.** 30 ounces   **D.** 20 milliliters

2. Which number best represents point Z on the number line? (*Circle the correct letter.*)

   A. 4.9

   B. 4.8

   C. 4.6

   D. 4.3

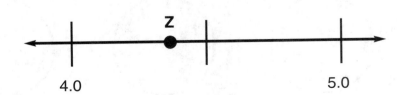

Name _____ **Date** _____

1. Mandy and Samantha each drew 2 shapes on the board. Samantha drew 2 congruent shapes. Mandy's shapes were not congruent. Fill in the table based on the drawings.

 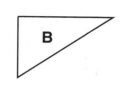

Drawings		
Name	**Shape**	
Samantha		
Mandy		

2. Which type of angle best represents the tip of the pencil? (*Circle the correct letter.*)

A. right angle

B. obtuse angle

C. acute angle

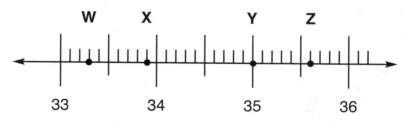

D. straight angle

Name _____ **Date** _____

1. What decimal represents point Z? (*Circle the correct letter.*)

A. 35.3

B. 33.9

C. 35

D. 35.6

W   X   Y   Z

33   34   35   36

2. How many sides does an octagon have? (*Circle the correct letter.*)

A. 8   **B.** 6   **C.** 4   **D.** 2

Name _____ **Date** _____

Warm-Up 41

1. Lisa drinks one cup of coffee in the morning before she goes to work. Which is the best estimate of the capacity of her coffee cup? (*Circle the correct letter.*)

A. 120 milliliters

C. 120 liters

B. 120 gallons

D. 120 centimeters

2. Which shape below is a pentagon? (*Circle the correct letter.*)

A. 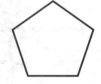　　**B.** 　　**C.** 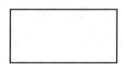　　**D.**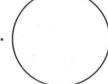

Name _____ **Date** _____

Warm-Up 42

1. Which thermometer shows the hottest temperature? (*Circle the correct letter.*)

A. 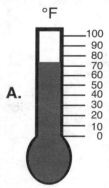　　**B.** 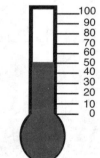　　**C.** 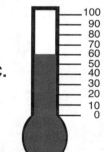　　**D.**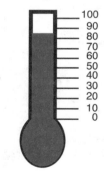

2. Use your ruler to measure the length of the paintbrush to the nearest inch. (*Circle the correct letter.*)

A. 4 inches　　**B.** 5 inches　　**C.** 6 inches　　**D.** 7 inches

DAILY Warm-Up 43

Name _____ Date _____

1. How many vertices, faces, and edges does a cube have? (*Circle the correct letter.*)

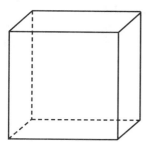

A. 12 edges, 8 faces, and 6 vertices

B. 6 faces, 12 vertices, and 8 edges

C. 12 edges, 8 vertices, and 6 faces

D. 8 faces, 6 vertices, and 12 faces.

2. Maci has a toy key. About how long is Maci's key?

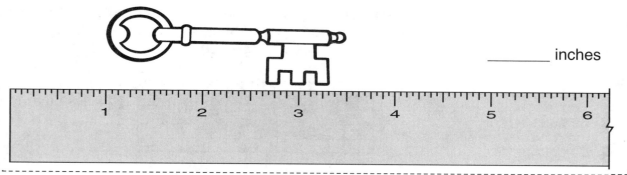

_____ inches

DAILY Warm-Up 44

Name _____ Date _____

1. Which figure is congruent to the shaded one? (*Circle the correct letter.*)

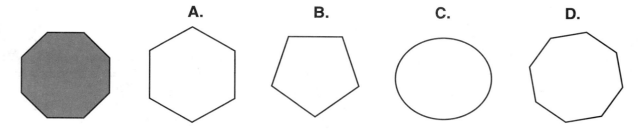

A.   **B.**   **C.**   **D.**

2. Which measurement best describes the length of a car? (*Circle the correct letter.*)

A. 12 inches   **B.** 12 feet   **C.** 12 meters   **D.** 12 centimeters

Name _____ **Date** _____

DAILY
Warm-Up 45

1. When Monica checked the temperature at 8:00 A.M., the temperature was 55°F. At 11:00 A.M., the temperature had risen 25 degrees. On the thermometer, shade the temperature at 11:00 A.M.

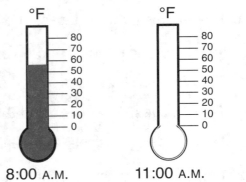

8:00 A.M.   11:00 A.M.

2. Garret needs new carpet for his living room. The shaded area is the shape of his living room. How many square feet of carpet does Garret need? (*Circle the correct letter.*)

A. 56 square feet

B. 58 square feet

C. 59 square feet

D. 60 square feet

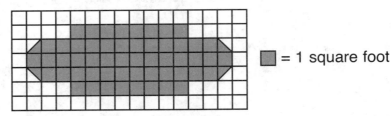

☐ = 1 square foot

Name _____ **Date** _____

DAILY
Warm-Up 46

1. Which pair of figures is congruent? (*Circle the correct letter.*)

A.   **B.**   **C.**   **D.**

2. Jack is buying a new bed. About how long is an average bed? (*Circle the correct letter.*)

A. 7 feet

B. 7 inches

C. 7 yards

D. 7 miles

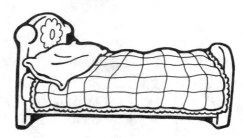

98   ©Teacher Created Resources, Inc.

DAILY Warm-Up 47

Name _____ Date _____

1. About how many feet tall is a door? (*Circle the correct letter.*)

   A. 2 feet   **B.** 4 feet   **C.** 7 feet   **D.** 12 feet

2. Terry is buying grapes for her son. About how much do the grapes weigh? (*Circle the correct letter.*)

   A. 140 grams

   B. 110 grams

   C. 120 grams

   D. 130 grams

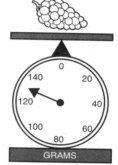

DAILY Warm-Up 48

Name _____ Date _____

1. Linda drew the following figures on the board. Which figure could be cut to make two triangles? (*Circle the correct letter.*)

   A.   **B.**   **C.**   **D.**

2. Chelsea will be at the gym by 6:00 P.M. The clock shows the time now. How many more minutes until she is at the gym?

   _____ more minutes

DAILY Warm-Up 49

Name _____ Date _____

1. Janice bought 2 pounds of apples. How many ounces are in 2 pounds? (*Circle the correct letter.*)

   A. 16 ounces   **B.** 32 ounces   **C.** 36 ounces   **D.** 48 ounces

2. John started mowing his lawn at 1:00. He finished 45 minutes later. Mark the time he finished on the clock below.

Started

Finished

DAILY Warm-Up 50

Name _____ Date _____

1. Which letter does not have a line of symmetry? (*Circle the correct letter.*)

   A. M   **B.** R   **C.** T   **D.** H

2. Mr. Hoover is a teacher. He made business cards to give to his students' parents. Use your ruler to measure the perimeter of the business card in inches. (*Circle the correct letter.*)

   A. 5 inches

   B. 6 inches

   C. 9 inches

   D. 10 inches

Mr. Hoover
4th Grade Teacher
Glenbrook Elementary
979-555-TEACH

DAILY

Warm-Up 51

Name _____

Date _____

1. Which pair of figures is congruent? (*Circle the correct letter.*)

A.

B.

C.

D.

2. How long is the pencil using the units below?

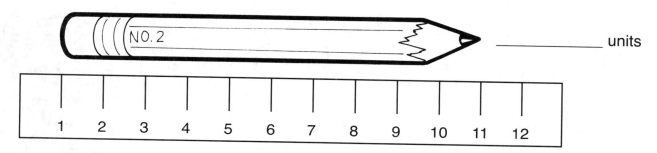

_____ units

DAILY

Warm-Up 52

Name _____

Date _____

1. Pete drew a circle inside a rectangle. Which example shows Pete's drawing? (*Circle the correct letter.*)

A. 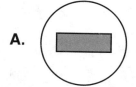   **B.** 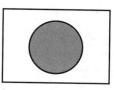   **C.**   **D.**

2. What unit of measurement would you use to count how long it would take a person to say the alphabet? (*Circle the correct letter.*)

A. seconds   **B.** minutes   **C.** hours   **D.** years

Name _____   **Date** _____

Warm-Up 53

1. Which is **not** true about a triangular prism? (*Circle the correct letter.*)

   A. It has 5 faces.

   B. It has 6 faces.

   C. It has 2 faces that are triangles.

   D. It has 3 faces that are rectangles.

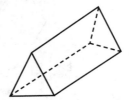

2. Which measuring cup shows $\frac{3}{4}$ of cup full? (*Circle the correct letter.*)

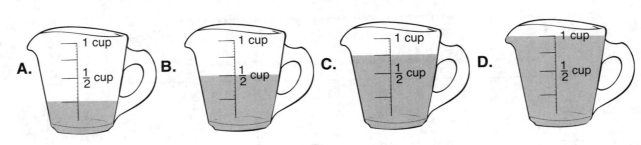

- -

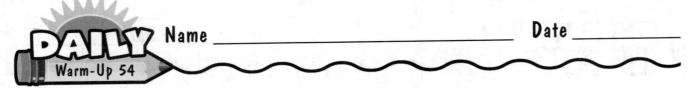

Name _____   **Date** _____

Warm-Up 54

1. Seth and Cane each drew a rectangle on a sheet of paper. Seth's rectangle was 8 centimeters long. How long is Cane's rectangle? (*Circle the correct letter.*)

   A. 4 centimeters

   B. 6 centimeters

   C. 8 centimeters

   D. 10 centimeters

2. Margo left work at 3:30 P.M. She arrived home 2 hours and 15 minutes later. Which clock shows the time Margo arrived home? (*Circle the correct letter.*)

   A.   **B.**   **C.**   **D.**

DAILY Warm-Up 55

Name _____ Date _____

1. Frank's birthday is November 30th. If today is November 4th, how many more days until Frank's birthday? (*Circle the correct letter.*)

November						
SUNDAY	MONDAY	TUESDAY	WEDNESDAY	THURSDAY	FRIDAY	SATURDAY
		1	2	3	4	5
6	7	8	9	10	11	12
13	14	15	16	17	18	19
20	21	22	23	24	25	26
27	28	29	30			

   A. 23   **C.** 25

   B. 24   **D.** 26

2. Robin has an earache. The doctor gave her drops to place in her ear twice a day. About how much medicine will Robin use in her ear each day? (*Circle the correct letter.*)

   A. 2 liters   **B.** 2 pints   **C.** 2 milliliters   **D.** 2 gallons

---

DAILY Warm-Up 56

Name _____ Date _____

1. Janice is measuring her backyard. What is the perimeter of the backyard? (*Circle the correct letter.*)

   A. 45 feet
   B. 25 feet
   C. 90 feet
   D. 500 feet

   20 ft. [rectangle] 25 ft.

2. Match the problems with the correct letters.

   _____ **1.** Which of these units can best be used to measure the width of your house?

   _____ **2.** Which of these units can best be used to measure the distance from one town to another?

   _____ **3.** Which of these units can best be used to measure the width of a dime?

   _____ **4.** Which of these units can best be used to measure the length of a pencil?

KEY
A = centimeters
B = meters
C = millimeters
D = kilometers

Name _____   **Date** _____

DAILY Warm-Up 57

1. Which is **true** about a rectangular prism? (*Circle the correct letter.*)

    A. It has 6 faces, two of which are triangular.

    B. It has 6 faces. All 6 faces are rectangles.

    C. It has fewer edges than a cube.

    D. It has 1 curved surface.

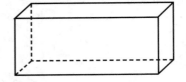

2. Write each shape name in the correct grid.

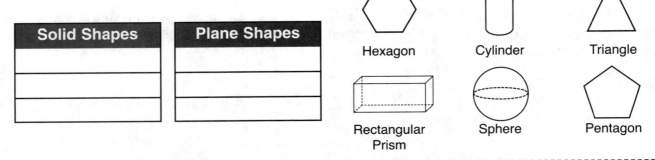

Solid Shapes	Plane Shapes

Hexagon   Cylinder   Triangle

Rectangular Prism   Sphere   Pentagon

Name _____   **Date** _____

DAILY Warm-Up 58

1. Yolanda is making photo albums for her 3 friends. She needs 2 ft. of lace for each of the photo albums. If she can only buy the lace in inches, how many inches of lace will she need for all three photo albums? (*Show your work and write your final answer on the line.*)

_____ inches

2. Today is April 4th. On April 29th, there is a school holiday. How many more days until the school holiday?

_____ more days

Name _____ **Date** _____

Warm-Up 59

1. Lee Ann is making a design out of squares. Each square equals 1 square inch. What is the area of the design Lee Ann is making? (*Circle the correct letter.*)

    A. 48 square inches

    B. 54 square inches

    C. 50 square inches

    D. 56 square inches

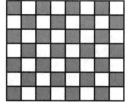

2. Jack is making a fenced area for his dog. The shaded part of the grid shows the fenced area. What is the area inside Jack's fence? (*Circle the correct letter.*)

    A. 22 square feet

    B. 32 square feet

    C. 42 square feet

    D. 52 square feet

    ▨ = 1 square foot

Name _____ **Date** _____

Warm-Up 60

1. Which of these units can best be used to measure the height of a tree? (*Circle the correct letter.*)

    A. kilometers   **C.** inches

    B. meters   **D.** centimeters

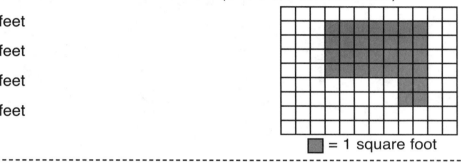

2. Which of these units can best be used to measure the weight of a candy bar? (*Circle the correct letter.*)

    A. grams   **B.** liters   **C.** pounds   **D.** milliliters

DAILY
Warm-Up 61

Name _____ Date _____

1. Look at these shapes. Decide whether each pair of shapes is congruent or not congruent.

A. 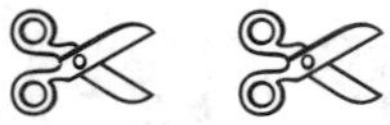  These shapes are _____.

B.  These shapes are _____.

C. 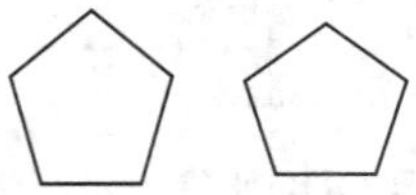 These shapes are _____.

2. Maria went to a movie at 2:20 P.M. The movie ended 2 hours and 20 minutes later. Mark the hands on the clock for the time the movie ended.

Started 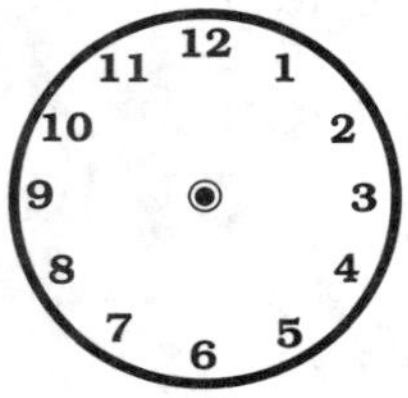   Ended

DAILY
Warm-Up 62

Name _____ Date _____

1. How many pints equal 1 gallon? (*Circle the correct letter.*)

A. 8   B. 6   C. 5   D. 4

2. Which figure is shown below? (*Circle the correct letter.*)

A. pentagon

B. hexagon

C. cube

D. cylinder

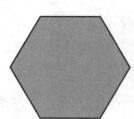

Warm-Up 1
1. B
2. C

Warm-Up 2
1. D
2. B

Warm-Up 3
1. C
2. A

Warm-Up 4
1. A. S
   B. S
   C. P
   D. P
   E. S
2. C

Warm-Up 5
1.

2. C

Warm-Up 6
1. C
2. D

Warm-Up 7
1. C
2. A

Warm-Up 8
1. A. 3; triangle
   B. 5; pentagon
   C. 6; hexagon
   D. 4; rectangle
2. A

Warm-Up 9
1. C
2. C

Warm-Up 10
1. 52 square feet
2. D

Warm-Up 11
1. B
2. B

Warm-Up 12
1. D
2. B

Warm-Up 13
1. C
2. No. The shape on the left is a cube. The shape on the right is a rectangular prism.

Warm-Up 14
1. A
2. A. Number of sides = 6
      Name of shape = hexagon
   B. Number of sides = 5
      Name of shape = pentagon
   C. Number of sides = 8
      Name of shape = octagon

Warm-Up 15
1. C
2.

Warm-Up 16
1. 80 feet
2. A

Warm-Up 17
1. C
2. No

Warm-Up 18
1. C
2. D

Warm-Up 19
1. D
2. B

Warm-Up 20
1. The lines are perpendicular because they make right angles where they intersect. Parallel lines never intersect.
2. 25 days

Warm-Up 21
1. A
2. 4 times

Warm-Up 22
1. C
2. D

Warm-Up 23
1. C
2. D

Warm-Up 24
1. A
2. 8 cm

Warm-Up 25
1. D
2. Alike

Warm-Up 26
1. B
2. A. 4 Mondays
   B. 30 days

Warm-Up 27
1. A and D
2.

Warm-Up 28
1. A
2. B

Warm-Up 29
1. C
2. A

Warm-Up 30
1. B
2.

Warm-Up 31
1. D
2. A. 4:40

   B. 5:30

   C. 12:00

   D. 9:25

Warm-Up 32
1. 7 cm
2. C

Warm-Up 33
1. D
2. D

Warm-Up 34
1. 24 inches
2. C

Warm-Up 35
1. The one on the left is a cube and the one on the right is a rectangular prism.
2. Parallel lines are correct if lines will never intersect. Perpendicular lines are correct if they intersect at 90° angles.

Warm-Up 36
1. A
2. B

Warm-Up 37
1. D
2. B

Warm-Up 38
1. B
2. D

Warm-Up 39
1. Samantha: A, D
   Mandy: B, C
2. C

Warm-Up 40
1. D
2. A

Warm-Up 41
1. A
2. A

Warm-Up 42
1. D
2. B

Warm-Up 43
1. C
2. $2\frac{1}{2}$ inches

Warm-Up 44
1. D
2. B

Warm-Up 45
1.
2. A

Warm-Up 46
1. B
2. A

Warm-Up 47
1. C
2. D

Warm-Up 48
1. C
2. 45 more minutes

Warm-Up 49
1. B
2.

Warm-Up 50
1. B
2. D

Warm-Up 51
1. B
2. 10 units

Warm-Up 52
1. B
2. A

Warm-Up 53
1. B
2. C

Warm-Up 54
1. A
2. D

Warm-Up 55
1. D
2. C

Warm-Up 56
1. C
2. 1 = B
   2 = D
   3 = C
   4 = A

Warm-Up 57
1. B
2.

Solid Shapes	Plane Shapes
Cylinder	Hexagon
Sphere	Triangle
Rectangular Prism	Pentagon

Warm-Up 58
1. 72 inches
2. 25 more days

Warm-Up 59
1. D
2. B

Warm-Up 60
1. B
2. A

Warm-Up 61
1. A. congruent
   B. congruent
   C. not congruent
2.

Warm-Up 62
1. A
2. B

GRAPHS, DATA AND PROBABILITY

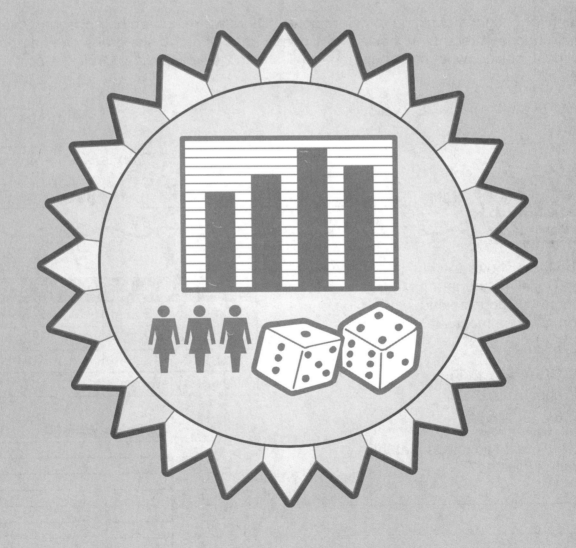

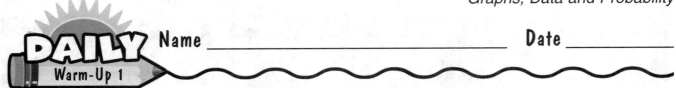

DAILY Warm-Up 1

Name _____   Date _____

1. The graph shows the number of pets each teacher has in her house. How many pets does Mrs. Robins have?

_____ pets

Pets Owned

Number of Pets

8
6
4
2
0

Ms. Long   Ms. Brooks   Mrs. Robins

Teachers

2. Jennifer bought a package of hair ribbons. There were 3 green hair ribbons, 2 yellow hair ribbons, 4 red hair ribbons, and 1 purple hair ribbon. If she grabs one hair ribbon without looking, what color hair ribbon will she most likely pick? (*Circle the correct letter.*)

A. green   **B.** yellow   **C.** red   **D.** purple

- -

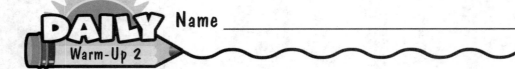

DAILY Warm-Up 2

Name _____   Date _____

1. The table shows the number of donuts Mr. Bozalina bought. If Mr. Bozalina takes 1 donut without looking, which type of donut will he most likely get?

A. glazed

B. strawberry swirl

C. chocolate

D. cream filled

Type of Donut	Number of Donuts
glazed	3
cream filled	2
chocolate	6
strawberry swirl	4

2. List at least two things that this graph indicates?

_____

_____

_____

_____

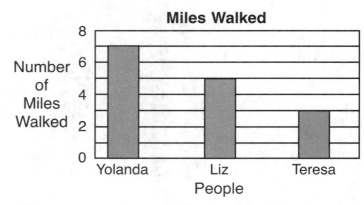

Miles Walked

Number of Miles Walked

8
6
4
2
0

Yolanda   Liz   Teresa

People

DAILY Warm-Up 3

Name _____ Date _____

1. Linda has a bag of cubes. If she reaches in without looking, what number cube will she most likely pick? How do you know?

_____

_____

_____

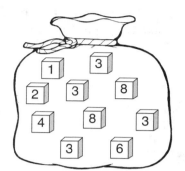

2. How many more letters altogether did Ty and Maci receive than Sally?

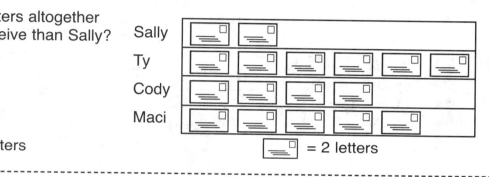

Sally	

_____ more letters

= 2 letters

DAILY Warm-Up 4

Name _____ Date _____

1. Jennifer and Hannah are playing a game. If Hannah spins the spinner, which color will the spinner most likely land on? (*Circle the correct letter.*)

A. Black   **C.** Green

B. Red   **D.** Blue

2. The table shows the number of sodas Wanda bought for a family picnic. If she reaches in the picnic basket without looking, what flavor of soda will she least likely pick?

Kind of Soda	vanilla	strawberry	cherry	grape	orange
Number of Sodas	3	2	7	5	6

She will least likely pick _____ soda.

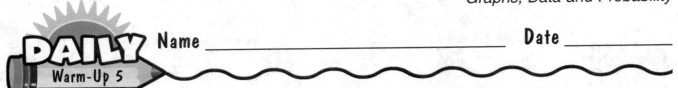

Name _____ **Date** _____

Warm-Up 5

1. Jeff is playing a number game with his brother. If Jeff spins the spinner, which number will it most likely land on? (*Circle the correct letter.*)

A. 1   **C.** 3

B. 2   **D.** 5

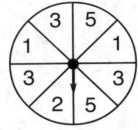

2. The table shows the number of shirts James has in his closet? If he reaches in the closet without looking, which answer shows the probability of selecting a blue shirt? (*Circle the correct letter.*)

Color of shirt	green	yellow	white	blue
Number of shirts	2	1	4	5

A. $\frac{1}{12}$ **B.** $\frac{2}{12}$ **C.** $\frac{4}{12}$ **D.** $\frac{5}{12}$

- -

Name _____ **Date** _____

Warm-Up 6

1. Use the information below to complete the graph.

Yellow	4
Blue	5
Red	3
Green	7
Orange	6

Colored Cubes

	1	2	3	4	5	6	7	8
Yellow								
Blue								
Red								
Green								
Orange								

2. The table shows the number of boxes a T-shirt company had on inventory. If an employee opens 1 box of T-shirts without looking, which size T-shirt is he or she least likely to get?

Size of T-shirts	Number of Boxes
Small	6
Medium	7
Large	4
Extra Large	2

_____ T-shirt

DAILY Warm-Up 7

Name _____ Date _____

1. If you flip a coin, it will either land on heads or tails. Circle your answer.

True   or   False

2. Students in Mrs. Watkin's class graphed the eye colors of their classmates. Answer the questions based on the table below.

How many more students have brown eyes than blue eyes?

_____ more students

How many students have blue, brown, and green eyes?

_____ students

Student Eye Color

= 2 children

DAILY Warm-Up 8

Name _____ Date _____

1. Use the graph to answer the questions.

How many cars in the parking lot were red?

_____ cars

How many red, green, and silver cars were there?

_____ cars

Color of Cars in Parking Lot

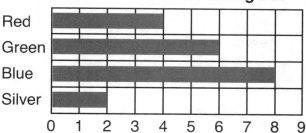

2. If Mrs. Harrison spins the spinner, what color will it most likely land on?

The color _____

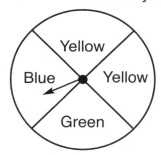

Name _____ **Date** _____

DAILY Warm-Up 9

1. Look at the spinner. Which tally chart shows the most likely results of 10 spins? (*Circle the correct letter.*)

A.

Number	Results
4	IIII
3	III
2	II
1	I

B.

Number	Results
4	�
3	I
2	III
1	II

C.

Number	Results
4	I
3	II
2	II
1	�

D.

Number	Results
4	I
3	�
2	II
1	II

2. Jeb has 3 orange hats, 2 green hats, 1 yellow hat, and 4 blue hats hanging in his closet. If he reaches in the closet without looking, which color hat will he least likely pick?

He will least likely pick a _____ hat.

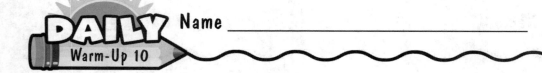

Name _____ **Date** _____

DAILY Warm-Up 10

1. Use the graph to answer the questions.

How many total ribbons did the boys earn altogether?

_____ ribbons

How many more ribbons did Sam and Ted earn than Lou and Gene?

_____ more ribbons

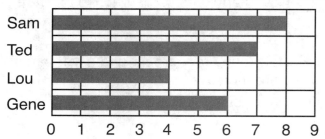

Number of 1st Place Ribbons Earned

2. What is the probability of landing on A?

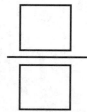

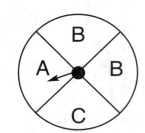

114

©Teacher Created Resources, Inc.

DAILY Warm-Up 11   Name _____   Date _____

1. Which of the following best describes the results of the table below? (*Circle the correct letter.*)

   A. Ted read the most pages.

   B. Jane read 3 more pages than Ted.

   C. Jane read 6 more pages than Ted.

   D. Ted read 6 more pages than Jane.

Number of Pages Read in One Day	
Ted	153
Jane	159

2. Gordon has 3 green shirts, 2 blue shirts, 1 yellow shirt, and 3 red shirts in his closet. If he grabs 1 shirt without looking, what is the probability he will select a red shirt? (*Circle the correct letter.*)

   A. $\frac{2}{10}$ **B.** $\frac{3}{9}$ **C.** $\frac{2}{9}$ **D.** $\frac{2}{6}$

DAILY Warm-Up 12   Name _____   Date _____

1. The table shows the number of baskets 4 students made playing basketball. Based on the table, how many baskets did Hank, David, and Jody make altogether?

Student Names	Baskets Made
Hank	3
Pete	2
David	6
Jody	4

   They made _____ baskets.

2. List at least two things that this graph indicates?

   _____
   _____
   _____
   _____
   _____
   _____

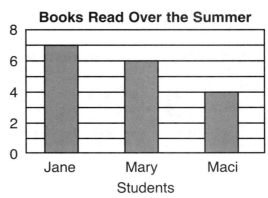

Books Read Over the Summer

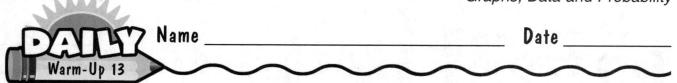

DAILY Warm-Up 13   Name _____   Date _____

1. Kathy has a box of colored cubes. The table shows the number of cubes of each color in the box. If Kathy takes 1 colored cube out of the box without looking, which color will she most likely pick? (*Circle the correct letter.*)

A. green

B. blue

C. pink

D. yellow

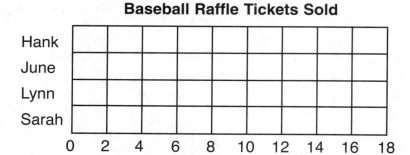

Color	pink	blue	green	yellow
Number	12	15	10	18

2. Complete the graph using the information below by shading in the squares.

Hank: ||||| ||

June: ||||| ||||| ||||| |

Lynn: ||||| ||||| ||

Sarah: ||||| ||||

Baseball Raffle Tickets Sold

Hank
June
Lynn
Sarah

0 2 4 6 8 10 12 14 16 18

- -

DAILY Warm-Up 14   Name _____   Date _____

1. Use the bar graph to answer the questions.

How many students voted for chocolate and chocolate chip as their favorite ice cream?

_____ students

How many students liked chocolate chip more than strawberry?

_____ students

Votes for Favorite Ice Cream

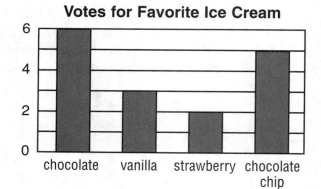

chocolate   vanilla   strawberry   chocolate chip

2. Which spinner is **least likely** to land on a 2? (*Circle the correct letter.*)

A.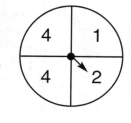

B.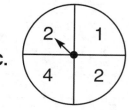

C.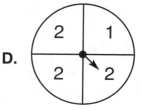

D.

DAILY Warm-Up 15

Name _____ Date _____

1. Mr. Franklin's class graphed the hair color of students in the class. The information below is the information they gathered. Use this information to complete the bar graph.

   Blonde: ||||| |||||

   Red: ||

   Brown: ||||| ||||| ||

   Black: ||||| ||||

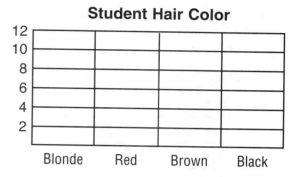

Student Hair Color

2. Lee has a box of rare coins. He has 3 quarters dated 1854, 6 pennies dated 1912, 4 nickels dated 1902, and 1 dime dated 1889. If he grabs 1 coin from the box without looking, what coin will he most likely pick? (*Circle the correct letter.*)

   A. nickel   **B.** quarter   **C.** penny   **D.** dime

DAILY Warm-Up 16

Name _____ Date _____

1. Use the bar graph to answer the questions.

   Who won the most card games?

   _____

   Who won the least card games?

   _____

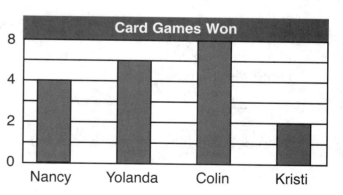

2. Which is **not** true about the spinner? (*Circle the correct letter.*)

   A. It will most likely land on a 1.

   B. There is a chance it will land on a 2.

   C. There is a chance it will land on a 4.

   D. There is a chance it will land on a 3.

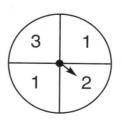

DAILY
Warm-Up 17

Name _____ Date _____

1. Complete the graph using the information below. Shade one square with your pencil for each tally mark.

Students Who Collected Cans	
Kathy	ⅡⅡⅡ Ⅱ
George	ⅡⅡⅡ Ⅰ
Ben	ⅡⅡⅡ
Beth	ⅡⅡⅡⅠ

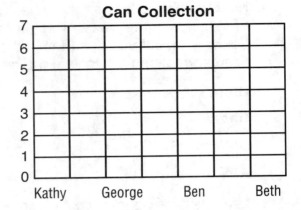

Can Collection

2. Elizabeth has 2 yellow pencils, 3 green pencils, 4 blue pencils, and 1 red pencil in her backpack. If she grabs 1 pencil without looking, what is the probability it will be a green pencil? (*Circle the correct letter.*)

A. $\frac{1}{10}$ B. $\frac{2}{10}$ C. $\frac{3}{10}$ D. $\frac{4}{10}$

DAILY
Warm-Up 18

Name _____ Date _____

1. Use the bar graph to answer the questions.

How many newspapers did Hank and Henry deliver?

_____ newspapers

Who delivered the most newspapers?

_____

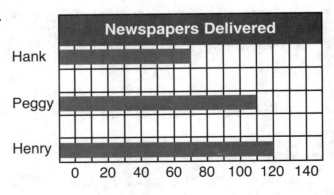

Newspapers Delivered

2. Jackie has 100 blocks numbered 1 through 3. If the spinner below shows the proportion of blocks numbered 1 through 3, how many blocks are numbered 1? (*Circle the correct letter.*)

A. 25   C. 75

B. 50   D. 100

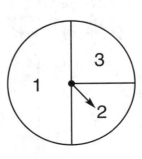

DAILY
Warm-Up 19

Name _____ **Date** _____

1. Complete the graph using the information below. Shade one square with your pencil for each tally mark.

Seashell Collection	
Mary	II
Linda	ℕℕ I
Joan	ℕℕ II
Jerry	IIII

Seashell Collection

	Mary	Linda	Joan	Jerry
7				
6				
5				
4				
3				
2				
1				
0				

2. Look at the pie graph. Which statement below is true? (*Circle the correct letter.*)

   A. More students like pizza than tacos.
   B. The number of students who like hamburgers and tacos are the same.
   C. More students like tacos than hamburgers.
   D. There are twice as many students who like hamburgers as there are students who like pizza.

Students' Favorite Foods

Pizza | Tacos

Hamburgers

DAILY
Warm-Up 20

Name _____ **Date** _____

1. Look at the graph.

   Which two teachers sold a total of 60 cameras altogether?

   _____ and _____

Cameras Sold

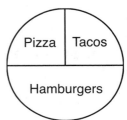

Mrs. Jones	📷 📷 📷
Mr. Cantu	📷
Mrs. Philips	📷 📷 📷 📷 📷
Mr. Simms	📷 📷 📷 📷 📷 📷

📷 = 10 cameras sold

2. Maxine has 3 quarters, 2 dimes, and 6 pennies in a box on her dresser. If she reaches in without looking, which coin will she most likely pick?

   Explain: _____

   _____

   _____

   _____

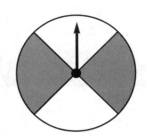

Name _____ **Date** _____

DAILY
Warm-Up 21

1. Use the spinner to answer the problem.

You have an even chance of landing on a shaded region.

Circle: **True**   or   **False**

2. Use the graph to answer the questions.

How many students have 1 phone
in their home?

_____ students

How many students have 3 phones
in their home?

_____ students

Number of Phones in Students' Homes

	☎		
	☎		☎
☎	☎	☎	☎
☎	☎	☎	☎
0 phones	1 phone	2 phones	3 phones

☎ = 2 students

- -

Name _____ **Date** _____

DAILY
Warm-Up 22

1. Nicole and Kelly are playing a game. If Nicole spins the spinner, which figure will it least likely land on? (*Circle the correct letter.*)

A. ✈

C. ✂

B. ✏

D. ❀

2. Pete has 3 blue toy cars, 1 green toy car, 2 yellow toy cars, and 4 red toy cars in his toy box. If he reaches in the toy box and grabs 1 toy car without looking, which color toy car will he most likely pick? (*Circle the correct letter.*)

A. blue   **B.** green   **C.** yellow   **D.** red

DAILY
Warm-Up 23

Name _____   Date _____

1. Use the information below to complete the graph.

Yellow	3
Blue	5
Red	4
Green	2
Orange	6

Color of Candy

	1	2	3	4	5	6	7	8
Yellow								
Blue								
Red								
Green								
Orange								

2. Circle *True* or *False* after each statement below.

It is unlikely that your teacher will bring a pet bear to school.   **True** or **False**

It is likely that you will work on a computer at school.   **True** or **False**

DAILY
Warm-Up 24

Name _____   Date _____

1. Circle *True* or *False* after each statement below.

It is likely that you will go swimming with a whale.   **True** or **False**

It is likely that your teacher will give homework this year.   **True** or **False**

2. Use the graph to answer the questions.

According to the graph, how many students like the color red?

_____ students

How many students like the colors green and yellow the best?

_____ students

Favorite Color

Blue	👤 👤 👤 ❘
Red	👤 👤 👤 👤
Green	👤 👤 ❘
Yellow	👤 👤 👤

👤 = 10 students

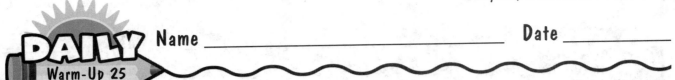

Name _____   **Date** _____

Warm-Up 25

1. The graph below shows the number of newspapers 3 friends delivered during the month of May. How many newspapers were delivered by Shane and Marie altogether?

_____ newspapers

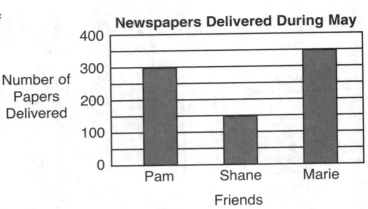

2. Samantha has 6 yellow dresses, 3 green dresses, 2 white dresses, and 1 orange dress hanging in her closet. If she grabs 1 dress without looking, what color dress will she least likely pick? (*Circle the correct letter.*)

A. green   **B.** yellow   **C.** white   **D.** orange

- -

Name _____   **Date** _____

Warm-Up 26

1. The table shows the color of envelopes on the left and the amount of each color on the right. If Mark grabs 1 envelope without looking, which color will he most likely grab? (*Circle the correct letter.*)

A. red   **C.** white

B. green   **D.** blue

Color of Envelopes	Number of Envelopes
red	3
green	2
white	6
blue	4

2. How many cars did Ben, Gene, and Will wash altogether?

_____ cars

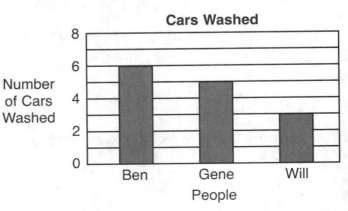

Name _____   **Date** _____

Warm-Up 27

1. Mr. Privitt loves reading. His books are all on a shelf in his living room. If he takes a book off the shelf without looking, which type of book will it most likely be? (*Circle the correct letter.*)

A. mystery

B. adventure

C. romance

D. history

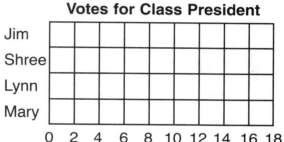

Type	mystery	adventure	romance	history
Number	6	7	2	4

2. Complete the graph using the information below.
(*Use your pencil to shade in the squares.*)

Jim: ⅢⅢ ⅢⅢ Ⅱ

Shree: ⅢⅢ ⅢⅢ ⅢⅢ Ⅰ

Lynn: ⅢⅢ ⅢⅢ Ⅱ

Mary: ⅢⅢ ⅢⅢ

Votes for Class President

Jim
Shree
Lynn
Mary

0 2 4 6 8 10 12 14 16 18

Name _____   **Date** _____

Warm-Up 28

1. Maria is playing a number game with her brother. If Maria spins the spinner, which number will it least likely land on? (*Circle the correct letter.*)

A. 1   **C.** 3

B. 2   **D.** 5

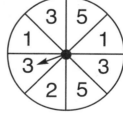

2. The table shows the number of colored cubes Darrel has in a box. If he reaches in the box without looking, which answer shows the probability of selecting a blue cube?
(*Circle the correct letter.*)

Color of Cubes	green	gold	white	blue
Number of Cubes	2	1	4	5

A. $\frac{1}{12}$ **B.** $\frac{2}{12}$ **C.** $\frac{4}{12}$ **D.** $\frac{5}{12}$

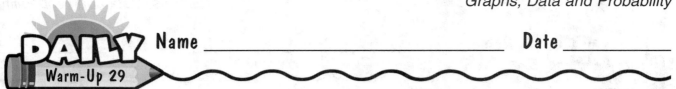

Name _____   Date _____

1. Jimmy has a box of candy. The table shows the flavors of candy in the box. If Jimmy takes 1 candy out of the box without looking, which flavor of candy will he most likely pick? (*Circle the correct letter.*)

   A. chocolate

   B. vanilla

   C. caramel

   D. peppermint

Color	chocolate	vanilla	caramel	peppermint
Number	12	15	10	18

2. Which is not true about the voting according to the graph? (*Circle the correct letter.*)

   A. Basketball received more votes than track.

   B. Track received more votes than tennis.

   C. Tennis received the least votes.

   D. Basketball received the most votes.

Votes for Favorite Sport	
Tennis	ꀤꀤ ꀤꀤ
Football	ꀤꀤ ꀤꀤ ꀤꀤ ꀤꀤ III
Basketball	ꀤꀤ ꀤꀤ ꀤꀤ ꀤꀤ I
Soccer	ꀤꀤ ꀤꀤ ꀤꀤ III
Track	ꀤꀤ ꀤꀤ II

Name _____   Date _____

1. The graph shows the number of couches available for sale at Hinojosa Wholesale.

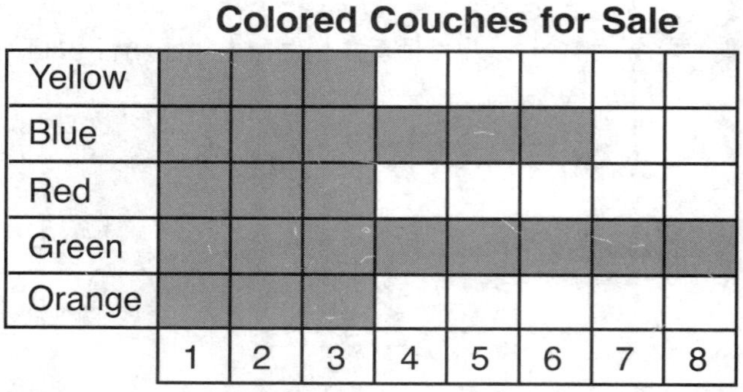

   How many couches are available for sale altogether?

   _____ couches

   How many couches altogether are green, red, and yellow?

   _____ couches

Colored Couches for Sale

	1	2	3	4	5	6	7	8
Yellow	▓	▓	▓					
Blue	▓	▓	▓		▓	▓		
Red	▓	▓	▓					
Green	▓	▓	▓					▓
Orange	▓	▓	▓					

2. The table shows the number of boxes of sweatshirts a graphics company had on inventory. If the boss opens 1 box of sweatshirts without looking, which size sweatshirt will he least likely get? (*Circle the correct letter.*)

   A. Small

   B. Medium

   C. Large

   D. Extra Large

Size of Sweatshirts	Number of Boxes
Small	6
Medium	7
Large	4
Extra Large	2

DAILY
Warm-Up 31

Name _____ Date _____

1. Circle *Possible* or *Not Possible* after each statement below.

   Before school you will brush your teeth.   **Possible** or **Not Possible**

   After school you will take your mom's car
   and go shopping.   **Possible** or **Not Possible**

2. Lilly has $2.00. She wants to buy 1 of the objects below. Which object will she least likely buy with her money? (*Circle the correct letter.*)

   A. Package of Pencils

   B. Scissors

   C. Comic Book

   D. Book of Stickers

Package of Pencils	Scissors	Comic Book	Book of Stickers
$1.56	**$1.25**	**$1.79**	**$2.10**

DAILY
Warm-Up 32

Name _____ Date _____

1. Four friends walk dogs for extra money. The chart below shows the number of dogs each friend walks. Use this information to complete the bar graph.

Sarah	3
Meredith	9
Cindy	8
Margaret	5

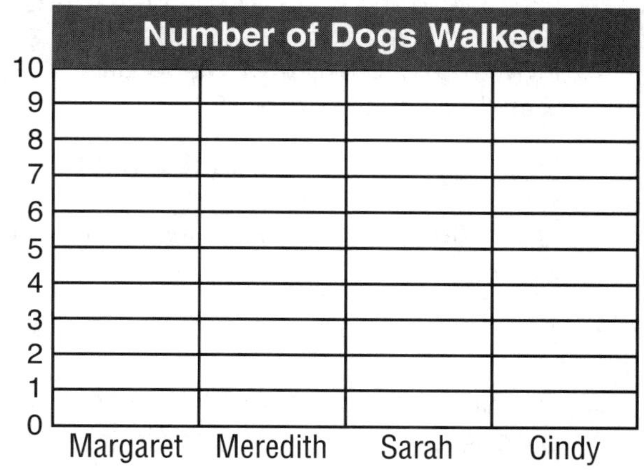

Number of Dogs Walked

10
9
8
7
6
5
4
3
2
1
0

Margaret   Meredith   Sarah   Cindy

2. Which of the activities will you probably not do on a snowy day? (*Circle the correct letter.*)

   A. build a snowman   **B.** wear a warm jacket   **C.** go swimming   **D.** sit by a fireplace

DAILY
Warm-Up 33

Name _____ Date _____

1. Use the bar graph to answer the questions.

At what hour were there the most customers?

_____ A.M.

How many total customers came in from
7:00 A.M. to 9:00 A.M.?

_____ customers

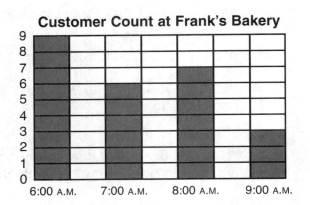

Customer Count at Frank's Bakery

2. Which spinner has the best chance of landing on a 4? (*Circle the correct letter.*)

A.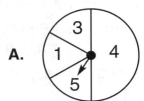

B.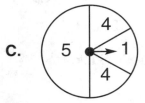

C.

- -

Graphs, Data and Probability

DAILY
Warm-Up 34

Name _____ Date _____

1. Use the bar graph to answer the questions.

How many computer discs did Joe, Nancy, and
Sandy use altogether?

_____ computer discs

How many more computer discs did Nancy and
Sandy use than Joe?

_____ more computer discs

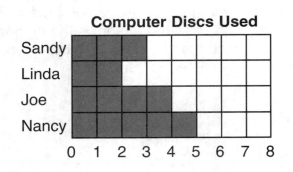

Computer Discs Used

2. Cassidy has 3 pieces of grape gum, 2 pieces of apple gum, 1 piece of lemon gum, and 4 pieces of strawberry gum in her pocket. If she grabs one piece of gum without looking, what flavor gum will she most likely pick? (*Circle the correct letter.*)

A. grape   **B.** apple   **C.** lemon   **D.** strawberry

DAILY Warm-Up 35

Name _____   Date _____

1. Circle *Possible* or *Not Possible* after each statement below.

   You will grow more than an inch this year.   **Possible** or **Not Possible**

   You will get sick and stay home from school.   **Possible** or **Not Possible**

2. Look at the graph.

   How many more ice-cream cones did Jack
   sell than Sam?

   _____ more ice-cream cones

   How many ice-cream cones did Jack and
   Sam sell altogether?

   _____ ice-cream cones

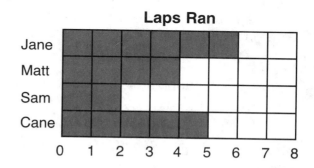

Ice-Cream Sales	
Jack	🍦🍦🍦🍦🍦🍦◺
Sam	🍦🍦🍦🍦

🍦 = 10 cones

- -

DAILY Warm-Up 36

Name _____   Date _____

1. Use the graph to answer the questions.

   Who ran fewer laps than Matt?

   _____

   Who ran more laps than Matt but
   fewer than Jane?

   _____

   Laps Ran

   (graph with rows Jane, Matt, Sam, Cane and axis 0 1 2 3 4 5 6 7 8)

2. Sue has a bag of buttons. She has 3 gold buttons, 2 yellow buttons, 4 blue buttons, and 1 white button. If she grabs one button without looking, what color button will she most likely pick? (*Circle the correct letter.*)

   A. gold   **B.** yellow   **C.** blue   **D.** white

DAILY Warm-Up 37

Name _____ **Date** _____

1. Which of the following best describes the results of the table below? (*Circle the correct letter.*)

   A. Frank worked the least amount of hours.

   B. Mary worked twice as many hours as Jan.

   C. Sam worked twice as many hours as Frank.

   D. Jan worked the most hours.

Employees	Hours Worked
Mary	26
Sam	34
Jan	13
Frank	54

2. Sherry has 2 green purses, 3 white purses, 1 yellow purse, and 4 orange purses hanging in her closet. If she grabs 1 purse without looking, what is the probability she will select a white purse? (*Circle the correct letter.*)

   A. $\frac{2}{10}$ **B.** $\frac{3}{9}$ **C.** $\frac{3}{10}$ **D.** $\frac{2}{10}$

DAILY Warm-Up 38

Name _____ **Date** _____

1. The table shows the number of apples 4 friends picked. Based on the table, how many apples did Shree, Lee, Brandi, and Gordon pick altogether?

   _____ apples

Names	Apples
Shree	34
Lee	56
Brandi	21
Gordon	67

2. According to the bar graph, how many ribbons did Dale and Tammy win?

   _____ ribbons

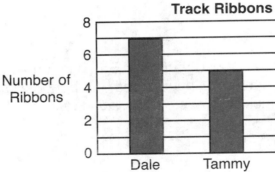

Name _____ **Date** _____

Warm-Up 39

1. Look at the spinner. Which tally chart shows the most likely results of 10 spins? (*Circle the correct letter.*)

A.

Number	Results
A	II
B	III
C	II
D	III

B.

Number	Results
A	IIII
B	II
C	II
D	I

C.

Number	Results
A	I
B	II
C	II
D	IIII

D.

Number	Results
A	I
B	IIII
C	II
D	II

2. Brandon caught 3 fish on Monday, 6 fish on Tuesday, 9 fish on Wednesday, and 12 fish on Thursday. If the pattern of fish caught continues, how many fish will Brandon catch on Friday?

_____ fish

- -

Name _____ **Date** _____

Warm-Up 40

1. Use the graph to answer the question.

   How many more cans did Sam and Ted recycle than Lou and Gene?

   _____ more cans

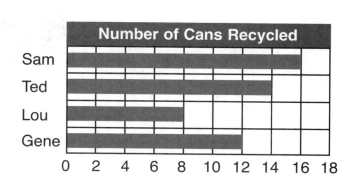

2. What is the probability of landing on a 3?

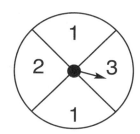

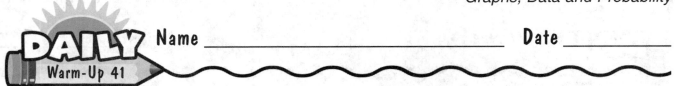

Name _____ **Date** _____

1. Travis spins the spinner 1 time. What is the probability of landing on a 2? (*Circle the correct letter.*)

A. likely

B. impossible

C. certain

D. unlikely

2. Charles has several small basketballs. Each basketball has a number printed on its side. Charles keeps the basketballs in a large box. If he reaches in the box and grabs 1 basketball without looking, what is the probability he will select a basketball with a 2 printed on it? (*Circle the correct letter.*)

A. $\frac{7}{7}$ **B.** $\frac{1}{7}$ **C.** $\frac{3}{7}$ **D.** $\frac{4}{7}$

Name _____ **Date** _____

1. Cassidy has many colored fish in her aquarium. If she reaches in with her net and catches 1 fish without looking, which color fish will she most likely catch?

_____ fish

Which color fish will she least likely catch?

_____ fish

Fish in Aquarium	
Green	13
Blue	18
Red	9
Yellow	15
Black	12

2. David has 3 pennies dated 1967, 4 pennies dated 1984, 5 pennies dated 1962, and 1 penny dated 2001 in his pocket. If he grabs 1 penny without looking, what date will the penny most likely be? (*Circle the correct letter.*)

A. 1967   **B.** 1984   **C.** 1962   **D.** 2001

1. Jeff is playing a number game with his brother. If Jeff spins the spinner, what is the probability it will land on a 3?

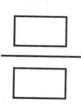

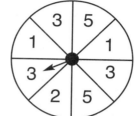

2. The table shows the number of necklaces Robin has in her jewelry box. If she reaches in without looking, which answer shows the probability of selecting a gold necklace? (*Circle the correct letter.*)

Color of necklaces	green	gold	white	blue
Number of necklaces	2	1	4	5

A. $\frac{1}{12}$ B. $\frac{2}{12}$ C. $\frac{4}{12}$ D. $\frac{5}{12}$

----

1. Mary has a box of geometric shapes. The table shows the number of different shapes in the box. If Mary takes 1 geometric shape out of the box without looking, which shape will she least likely pick? (*Circle the correct letter.*)

   A. cube

   B. cylinder

   C. sphere

   D. triangle

Shape	cube	cylinder	sphere	triangle
Number	12	23	11	18

2. Complete the graph using the information below. (*Use your pencil to shade in the squares.*)

   Lee: ||||| ||||

   Terry: ||||| ||||| |||||

   Heath: ||||| |||||

   Robin: ||||| ||||| |

Hours Worked

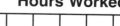

Lee

Terry

Heath

Robin

0 2 4 6 8 10 12 14 16 18

DAILY
Warm-Up 45

Name _____ **Date** _____

1. Use the bar graph to answer the questions.

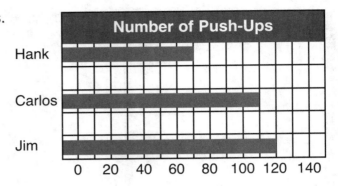

Number of Push-Ups

How many push-ups did Hank and Carlos do altogether?

_____ push-ups

How many more push-ups must Hank do to reach 100?

_____ more push-ups

2. Jackie has 100 beads. The beads are red, blue, or green. How many beads are green according to the pie graph? (*Circle the correct letter.*)

A. 25   **C.** 75

B. 50   **D.** 100

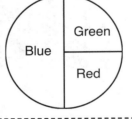

- -

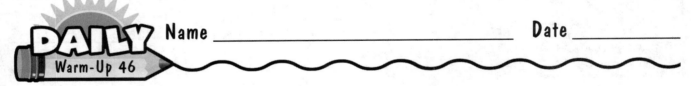

DAILY
Warm-Up 46

Name _____ **Date** _____

1. Circle *Likely* or *Unlikely* after each statement below.

You will gain weight this year.   **Likely** or **Unlikely**

You will get an upset stomach if you eat too much candy.   **Likely** or **Unlikely**

2. Marsha has 3 green ink pens, 2 blue ink pens, 1 red ink pen, and 5 black ink pens in her purse. If she reaches in without looking, which color ink pen will she most likely pick? Explain your answer.

_____

_____

_____

_____

Name _____ **Date** _____

DAILY Warm-Up 47

1. What number will the spinner most likely land on?
(*Circle the correct letter.*)

A. 1   **C.** 3

B. 2   **D.** 4

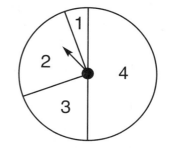

2. Use the graph to answer the questions.

How many miles ridden does each  equal?

_____ miles

How many more miles did Sarah and Scott
ride than Jody and Cassidy?

_____ more miles

Miles Ridden on Bikes	
Jody	🚲 🚲 🚲
Scott	🚲 🚲|
Cassidy	🚲
Sarah	🚲 🚲 🚲 🚲

🚲 = 20 miles

Name _____ **Date** _____

DAILY Warm-Up 48

1. Use the bar graph to answer the questions below.

How many more newspaper subscriptions
altogether did Karen and Debbie sell than Mark?

_____ more subscriptions

Who sold more subscriptions than
Eric but less than Mark?

_____

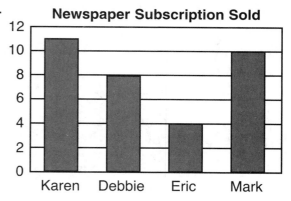

Newspaper Subscription Sold

2. Consider what might happen during a regular school day.

You will have math homework this week.   Circle: **Likely** or **Unlikely**

Your teacher will do your homework.   Circle: **Likely** or **Unlikely**

DAILY
Warm-Up 49

Name _____   Date _____

1. Carlos, Isaac, Kim, and Janet all entered a race. Carlos is the slowest runner. Isaac is a faster runner than Kim but a slower runner than Janet. List the order the runners will probably finish from fastest to slowest. (*Circle the correct letter.*)

   A. Janet   Isaac   Kim   Carlos

   B. Isaac   Janet   Kim   Carlos

   C. Carlos   Kim   Isaac   Janet

   D. Isaac   Kim   Janet   Carlos

2. Bryan, Tammy, Rick, and Laurie are brothers and sisters. Bryan is older than Rick but younger than Tammy. Laurie is the oldest. Which list shows their order from youngest to oldest? (*Circle the correct letter.*)

   A. Bryan   Rick   Tammy   Laurie

   B. Rick   Bryan   Tammy   Laurie

   C. Rick   Tammy   Bryan   Laurie

   D. Laurie   Tammy   Bryan   Rick

DAILY
Warm-Up 50

Name _____   Date _____

1. Use the graph to answer the questions.

Which color marble does Jake have the most of?

_____

How many more blue and green marbles does Jake have than red and silver?

_____ more marbles

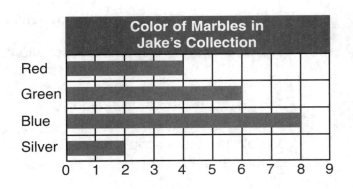

Color of Marbles in Jake's Collection

2. If Mrs. Harrison spins the spinner, what number will the spinner most likely land on?

The number _____

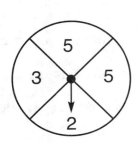

DAILY
Warm-Up 51

Name _____   Date _____

1. Look at the bar graph. If Pete swims 5 more laps, how many laps will he have swam? (*Circle the correct letter.*)

A. 4   **C.** 9

B. 5   **D.** 14

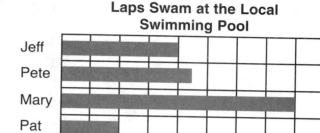

Laps Swam at the Local Swimming Pool

2. On Monday, Sam read 3 pages of his book. On Tuesday, he read 9 pages, and on Wednesday, he read 15 pages. If the pattern of pages read continues, how many pages will Sam read on Friday?

_____ pages

- -

DAILY
Warm-Up 52

Name _____   Date _____

1. Circle *Likely* or *Unlikely* after each statement below.

You will eat an apple this year.   **Likely** or **Unlikely**

You will eat a million apples this year.   **Likely** or **Unlikely**

2. Use the graph to answer the questions. How many students chose ice cream as their favorite snack?

_____ students

How many students chose cookies or apples as their favorite snacks?

_____ students

Students' Favorite Snacks

Cookie	👤	👤	👤	👤	👤		
Apple	👤	👤	👤	👤			
Chips	👤	👤	👤				
Ice Cream	👤	👤	👤	👤	👤	👤	👤

👤 = 10 students

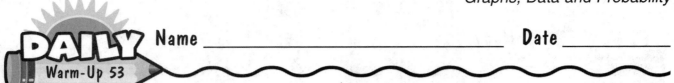

Name _____ Date _____

1. Linda has a bag of cubes. If she reaches in without looking, what number cube will she least likely pick? How do you know?

_____

_____

_____

_____

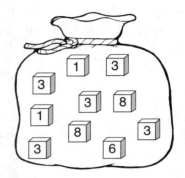

2. Look at the graph. Which 2 students received a total of 80 birthday cards?

_____ and _____

Sandy					
Tyler					
Courtney					
Matthew					

= 10 Birthday Cards

Name _____ Date _____

1. Look at the spinner. Which color will the spinner probably land on?

Explain: _____

_____

_____

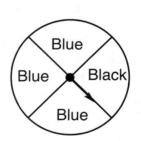

2. The table shows the number of juice boxes Wanda bought for a family picnic. If she reaches in without looking, what flavor of juice will she least likely pick?

Flavor	pineapple	carrot	apple	grape	orange
Number	3	2	7	5	6

She will least likely pick _____ juice.

DAILY Warm-Up 55

Name _____ Date _____

1. The graph shows the students in Mrs. Goldstein's class' favorite rides.

Which ride was most liked?

_____

How many students liked the Megatron, Ferris Wheel, or Spinner the best?

_____ students

Favorite Rides at the Fair

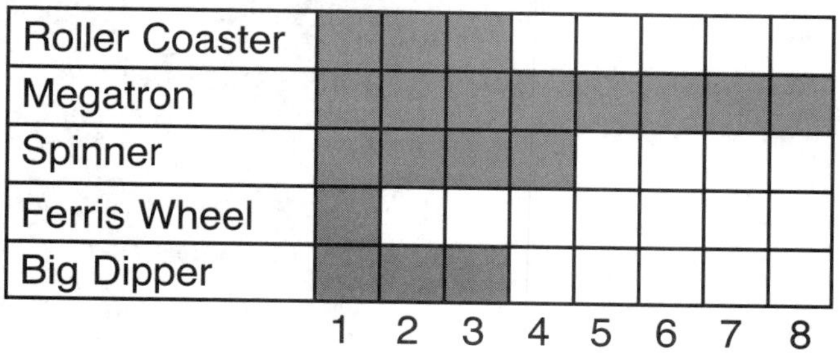

	1	2	3	4	5	6	7	8
Roller Coaster	▓	▓	▓					
Megatron	▓	▓	▓	▓	▓	▓	▓	▓
Spinner	▓	▓	▓	▓				
Ferris Wheel	▓							
Big Dipper	▓	▓	▓					

2. Look at the menu. Heather has $4.00 to spend on her lunch. What 2 items on the menu can she purchase without spending more money than she has? (*Circle the correct letter.*)

A. Cheeseburger and Shake
B. Apple Pie and Shake
C. Pizza Slice and Shake
D. Cheeseburger and Pizza Slice

Jack's Snack Attack Menu	
Cheeseburger	$4.35
Pizza Slice	$1.50
Apple Pie	$2.50
Shake	$2.00

DAILY Warm-Up 56

Name _____ Date _____

1. Susan has 2 pairs of white shoes, 3 pairs of brown shoes, 4 pairs of red shoes, and 1 pair of black shoes in her closet. If she grabs one pair of shoes without looking, which color shoes will she most likely pick?

Explain:_____

_____

_____

2. The graph shows the number of pets owned by 4th graders at Greentown Elementary. Use the graph to answer the following questions.

How many children does each 🐕 represent?

_____ children

How many children have 3 or more pets?

_____ children

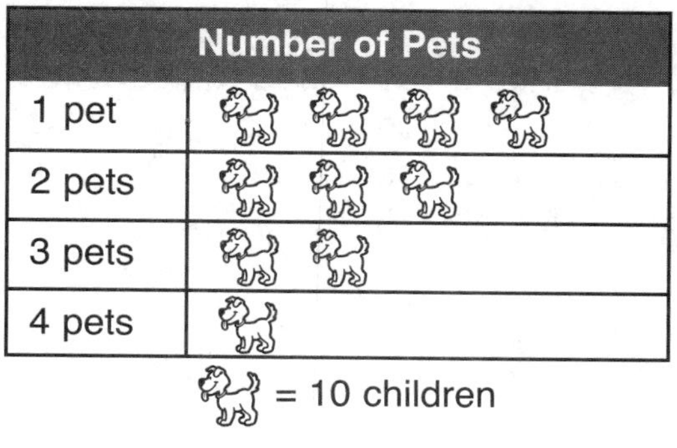

Number of Pets	
1 pet	🐕 🐕 🐕 🐕
2 pets	🐕 🐕 🐕
3 pets	🐕 🐕
4 pets	🐕

🐕 = 10 children

Name _____ **Date** _____

Warm-Up 57

1. The graph shows the number of students who rode their bikes to school last week.

   Which day did the most students bike to school?

   _____

   Which day do you think the weather was bad?

   _____

Number of Bike Riders

Monday						
Tuesday						
Wednesday						
Thursday						
Friday						
	1	2	3	4	5	6

2. Look at the price list. Samantha has $1.00. What 2 items can she buy that will equal $1.00? (*Circle the correct letter.*)

   A. Package of paper and a Large Eraser

   B. Pencil and Glue

   C. Large Eraser and Glue

   D. Pencil and a Package of Paper

Sam's School House	
Package of Paper	$1.50
Pencil	25¢
Large Eraser	15¢
Glue	75¢

Name _____ **Date** _____

Warm-Up 58

1. Look at the spinner. Is the chance of spinning an odd number likely, unlikely, certain, or impossible? (*Circle the correct letter.*)

   A. likely   **C.** certain

   B. unlikely   **D.** impossible

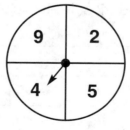

2. The graph shows the amount of money each class raised for new gym equipment. Mr. Jackson's class raised $20 and Mrs. Stolks class raised $30. How much money did Mrs. Burger's class raise?

   _____ dollars

Money Raised for Gym Equipment	
Mr. Jackson	$ $
Mr. Caldwell	$ $ $ $ $ $
Mrs. Burger	$ $ $ $ $
Mrs. Stolks	$ $ $

$ = 10 dollars

Warm-Up 59

1. Travis has 28 baseball cards and 18 football cards. What information is needed to find the number of baseball cards that are **not** dated before 2000? (*Circle the correct letter.*)

    A. the total number of football cards

    B. the number of baseball cards that are dated before 2000

    C. the number of football cards that are dated before 2000

    D. how much money each card is worth

2. The table shows the height of three students. Which number sentence can be used to find how many inches taller Lewis is than Tracy? (*Circle the correct letter.*)

    A. $56 - 52 =$ ☐

    B. $56 + 52 =$ ☐

    C. $56 + 48 =$ ☐

    D. $56 - 48 =$ ☐

Student	Height in Inches
Lewis	56 inches
Tracy	48 inches
Shawn	52 inches

Name _____ Date _____

Warm-Up 60

1. The tally chart shows the number of bracelets Abigail has in her jewelry box. If she takes 1 bracelet out without looking, what color bracelet will she most likely pick?

    _____

Bracelets in Jewelry Box

Color	Number
Red	ⅢⅡ II
Green	ⅢⅡ
Yellow	ⅢⅡ IIII
Orange	ⅢⅡ III

2. James made the number cards below and placed them in a dish. If he selects 1 card without looking, which card will he most likely pick? (*Circle the correct letter.*)

    | 3 | 1 | 2 | 3 | 4 | 4 | 2 | 3 | 3 | 4 |

    A. 1   **B.** 2   **C.** 3   **D.** 4

DAILY Warm-Up 61

Name _____   Date _____

1. The table shows the number of cans collected by 4 students. Which student collected more than 163 cans but less than 176? (*Circle the correct letter.*)

   A. Fred   **C.** Trisha

   B. Dominic   **D.** Heather

Cans Collected

Students	Number
Fred	163
Dominic	167
Trisha	176
Heather	159

2. Look at the table. Which statement is true? (*Circle the correct letter.*)

   A. Calley read more pages than Chelsea.

   B. Chelsea read an odd number of pages.

   C. Calley read an even number of pages.

   D. Chelsea read an even number of pages.

Pages Read

Calley	345
Chelsea	354

DAILY Warm-Up 62

Name _____   Date _____

1. What letter will the spinner most likely land on? (*Circle the correct letter.*)

   A. A   **C.** C

   B. B   **D.** D

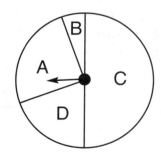

2. Use the graph to answer the question.

   If Jody rode 30 miles and Sarah rode 40 miles, how many miles did Scott ride?

   _____ miles

Miles Ridden on Bikes	
Jody	🚲 🚲 🚲
Scott	🚲 🚲
Cassidy	🚲
Sarah	🚲 🚲 🚲 🚲

Warm-Up 1
1. 7 pets
2. C

Warm-Up 2
1. C
2. Answers will vary.

Warm-Up 3
1. The number 3. There are more cubes with a 3.
2. 18 more letters

Warm-Up 4
1. D
2. strawberry

Warm-Up 5
1. C
2. D

Warm-Up 6
1.
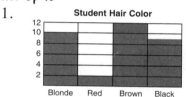
2. Extra Large

Warm-Up 7
1. True
2. 4 more students; 26 students

Warm-Up 8
1. 4 cars; 12 cars
2. Yellow

Warm-Up 9
1. A
2. yellow

Warm-Up 10
1. 25 ribbons; 5 more ribbons
2. $\frac{1}{4}$

Warm-Up 11
1. C
2. B

Warm-Up 12
1. 13 baskets
2. Answers will vary.

Warm-Up 13
1. D
2.
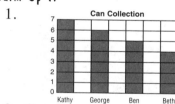

Warm-Up 14
1. 11 students; 3 students
2. B

Warm-Up 15
1.
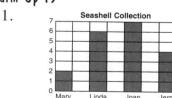
2. C

Warm-Up 16
1. Colin; Kristi
2. C

Warm-Up 17
1.

Can Collection

2. C

Warm-Up 18
1. 190 newspapers; Henry
2. B

Warm-Up 19
1.

Seashell Collection

2. D

Warm-Up 20
1. Mrs. Phillips and Mr. Cantu
2. She will most likely pick a penny because there are more of them.

Warm-Up 21
1. True
2. 8 students; 6 students

Warm-Up 22
1. C
2. D

Warm-Up 23
1.
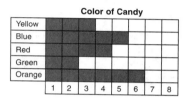
2. True; True

Warm-Up 24
1. False; True
2. 40 students; 55 students

Warm-Up 25
1. 500 newspapers
2. D

Warm-Up 26
1. C
2. 14 cars

Warm-Up 27
1. B
2.

Votes for Class President

Warm-Up 28
1. B
2. D

Warm-Up 29
1. D
2. D

Warm-Up 30
1. 23 couches; 14 couches
2. D

Warm-Up 31
1. Possible; Not Possible
2. D

Warm-Up 32
1.
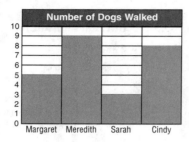
2. C

Warm-Up 33
1. 6:00 A.M.; 16 customers
2. A

Warm-Up 34
1. 12 computer discs; 4 more computer discs
2. D

Warm-Up 35
1. Possible; Possible
2. 25 more ice-cream cones; 105 ice-cream cones

Warm-Up 36
1. Sam; Cane
2. C

Warm-Up 37
1. B
2. C

Warm-Up 38
1. 178 apples
2. 12 ribbons

Warm-Up 39
1. B
2. 15 fish

Warm-Up 40
1. 10 more cans
2. $\frac{1}{4}$

Warm-Up 41
1. A
2. C

Warm-Up 42
1. Blue; Red
2. C

Warm-Up 43
1. $\frac{3}{8}$
2. A

Warm-Up 44
1. C
2.
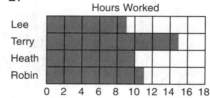

Warm-Up 45
1. 180 push-ups; 30 more push-ups
2. A

Warm-Up 46
1. Likely; Likely
2. She will most likely pick a black ink pen because there are more black ink pens than green, blue, or red.

Warm-Up 47
1. D
2. 20 miles; 30 more miles

Warm-Up 48
1. 9 more subscriptions; Debbie
2. Likely; Unlikely

Warm-Up 49
1. A
2. B

Warm-Up 50
1. Blue; 8 more marbles
2. 5

Warm-Up 51
1. D
2. 27 pages

Warm-Up 52
1. Likely; Unlikely
2. 70 students; 90 students

Warm-Up 53
1. Linda will least likely pick the number 6 cube because there is only one number 6 cube in the bag.
2. Courtney and Matthew

Warm-Up 54
1. The color blue because ¾ of the spinner is blue.
2. carrot

Warm-Up 55
1. Megatron; 13 students
2. C

Warm-Up 56
1. Susan will most likely pick a red pair of shoes because she has more red shoes than any other color.
2. 10 children; 30 children

Warm-Up 57
1. Thursday; Tuesday
2. B

Warm-Up 58
1. A
2. 50 dollars

Warm-Up 59
1. B
2. D

Warm-Up 60
1. Yellow
2. C

Warm-Up 61
1. B
2. D

Warm-Up 62
1. C
2. 15 miles

ALGEBRA, PATTERNS AND FUNCTIONS

DAILY
Warm-Up 1

Name _____   Date _____

1. Travis has a bag of small basketballs. He wants to divide them equally with his friends. If he counted the basketballs by 3s, which pattern shows how he counted them? (*Circle the correct letter.*)

   A. 3, 6, 10, 12

   B. 3, 6, 8, 12

   C. 3, 6, 9, 12

   D. 3, 8, 12, 15

2. Fill in the missing number in the box below.

22, 27, 32, 37, 42, ☐

DAILY
Warm-Up 2

Name _____   Date _____

1. Jason walked 2 miles on Monday, 4 miles on Tuesday, and 6 miles on Wednesday. If this pattern continues, how many miles will Jason walk on Friday?

   _____ miles

2. The table below shows the number of donuts in different numbers of packages. How many donuts are in 5 packages? (*Circle the correct letter.*)

   A. 15   **C.** 14

   B. 20   **D.** 17

Number of Packages	Number of Donuts
1	3
2	6
3	9
4	12
5	
6	18

DAILY Warm-Up 3

Name _____ Date _____

1. Mr. Hedgers plans to buy 4 pencils for each student who shows up for a Chess Club meeting. Which table below correctly shows how many pencils he will need to buy if 2, 4, 6, or 8 students show up for the meeting? (*Circle the correct letter.*)

A.

# of Students	Pencils Needed
2	6
4	8
6	10
8	12

B.

# of Students	Pencils Needed
2	8
4	8
6	24
8	32

C.

# of Students	Pencils Needed
2	8
4	16
6	24
8	32

D.

# of Students	Pencils Needed
2	8
4	10
6	24
8	32

2. Kirk is making bracelets with an equal number of colored beads on each bracelet. The table shows the number of colored beads he will need for different numbers of bracelets. Fill in the number of colored beads Kirk will need for 6 bracelets.

Number of Bracelets	Number of Colored Beads
2	20
3	30
4	40
5	50
6	

DAILY Warm-Up 4

Name _____ Date _____

1. The table shows the number of pencils in different numbers of packages. Fill in the number of pencils that are in 5 packages.

Number of Packages	Number of Pencils
1	6
2	12
3	18
4	24
5	

2. Write four number sentences for the numbers 2, 6, and 12.

_____ X _____ = _____   _____ ÷ _____ = _____

_____ X _____ = _____   _____ ÷ _____ = _____

DAILY Warm-Up 5

Name _____ Date _____

1. The table shows the number of tires on different numbers of bikes. Based on this pattern, how many tires are on 6 bikes?

Number of Bikes	Number of Tires
2	4
3	6
4	8
5	10
6	

2. Alexander made this pattern out of shapes. If Alexander continues this pattern, which 2 shapes will come next? (*Circle the correct letter.*)

A. ♣ ♦   **B.** ♣ ♣   **C.** ♦ ♥   **D.** ♥ ♣

DAILY Warm-Up 6

Name _____ Date _____

1. Mr. Withers bought a book of stickers to use on his students' work. Which expression shows how to find the total number of stickers on each sheet? (*Circle the correct letter.*)

A. 7 x 4   **C.** 4 x 8

B. 5 x 8   **D.** 8 x 8

2. Fill in the missing number. How did you find it?

70	61	52		34	25

_____

_____

_____

Name _____ **Date** _____

DAILY
Warm-Up 7

1. Mary drew a pattern on the chalkboard. She challenged her friend to find the missing shapes in the pattern. What shapes are missing? (*Circle the correct letter.*)

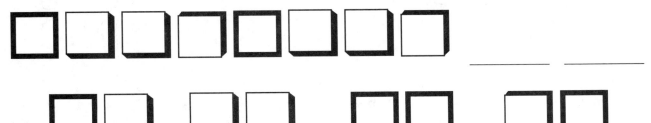

A. **B.** **C.** **D.**

2. Which number sentence is in the same fact family as 5 x 8 = 40? (*Circle the correct letter.*)

A. 8 − 5 = 3   **B.** 8 + 5 = 13   **C.** 40 ÷ 5 = 8   **D.** 40 − 5 = 35

Name _____ **Date** _____

DAILY
Warm-Up 8

1. Yolanda has a bag of shapes. Yolanda counted the shapes in groups of 6. Which pattern shows how she counted them? (*Circle the correct letter.*)

A. 12, 18, 24, 35   **C.** 6, 12, 15, 18

B. 6, 12, 18, 24   **D.** 6, 10, 14, 18

2. Look at the T-chart. Explain how the "IN" and "OUT" numbers are related.

_____

_____

_____

_____

IN	OUT
2	8
3	12
4	16
5	20
6	24

DAILY Warm-Up 9   Name _____   Date _____

1. Cody arranged some water bottles in the pattern shown to the right. Which operation best shows how he arranged them? (*Circle the correct letter.*)

   A. 6 − 4   **C.** 6 + 4

   B. 6 x 4   **D.** 6 + 5

2. Which number sentence is in the same family as 16 ÷ 8 = 2? (*Circle the correct letter.*)

   A. 16 − 8 = 8   **B.** 16 + 8 = 24   **C.** 16 x 2 = 32   **D.** 8 x 2 = 16

DAILY Warm-Up 10   Name _____   Date _____

1. Jennifer bought bananas at the store. The bananas came in bunches of 4. Which pattern shows how Jennifer would count the bunches by 4s? (*Circle the correct letter.*)

   A. 4, 8, 12, 15   **C.** 4, 9, 12, 16

   B. 4, 8, 11, 16   **D.** 4, 8, 12, 16

2. Look at the T-chart. Explain how the "IN" and "OUT" numbers are related.

IN	OUT
6	12
7	14
8	16
9	18
10	20

_____

_____

_____

_____

Name _____ **Date** _____

1. Draw the missing shape in the pattern below.

2. Write the missing number in the box that will make each number sentence true.

A. 6 x 4 = 3 x ☐   **D.** 4 x 4 = 2 x ☐   **G.** 3 x 2 = 2 x ☐

B. 5 x 2 = 1 x ☐   **E.** 2 x 6 = 3 x ☐   **H.** 2 x 7 = 7 x ☐

C. 5 x 1 = 1 x ☐   **F.** 6 x 3 = 2 x ☐   **I.** 3 x 3 = 9 x ☐

- -

Name _____ **Date** _____

1. Look at the table below.

In	11	10	9	8	7	6
Out	6	5	4	3	2	1

What is being done to the "In" numbers to get the "Out" numbers? _____

_____

_____

2. On 1 bike, there are 2 tires. On 2 bikes, there are 4 tires, and on 3 bikes there are 6 tires. Fill in the number of tires there are on 10 bikes.

Number of Bikes	1	2	3	4	5	6	7	8	9	10
Number of Tires	2	4	6	8	10	12	14	16	18	

Warm-Up 13

1. Write the missing number in the box that will make each number sentence true.

A. 6 x 3 = 2 x ☐   **D.** 4 x 4 = 2 x ☐   **G.** 9 x 2 = 1 x ☐

B. 6 x 4 = 3 x ☐   **E.** 7 x 3 = 3 x ☐   **H.** 2 x 3 = 6 x ☐

C. 2 x 6 = 6 x ☐   **F.** 2 x 4 = 8 x ☐   **I.** 6 x 2 = 3 x ☐

2. If the heart represents "A" and the rectangle represents "B", draw an AABAABAAB pattern using the figures below.

_____ _____ _____ _____ _____ _____ _____ _____ _____

Name _____ Date _____

Warm-Up 14

1. Fill in the following numbers that are missing in the pattern.

4, 4, 4, 5, 6, 5, 5, 5, 6, 7, 6, 6, 6, _____ , _____

2. On Monday, Alfred walked 2 miles. On Tuesday, he walked 4 miles, and on Wednesday, he walked 6 miles. If the pattern of miles walked continues, how many miles will Alfred walk on Thursday?

_____ miles

Name _____ **Date** _____

1. Craig went to a sports store to buy tennis balls. The tennis balls came in containers of 3. If you don't know how many containers Craig bought, which answer could be the total number of tennis balls Craig purchased? (*Circle the correct letter.*)

A. 4   **C.** 10

B. 8   **D.** 12

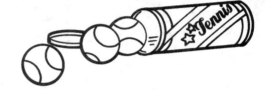

2. Marshal wrote a pattern of numbers on the board. He asked his friend to find the missing number. Fill in the missing number for Marshal.

18, 24, 30, 36, 42, ☐

Name _____ **Date** _____

1. Sasha swims laps in her swimming pool each morning. On Monday, she swam 3 laps. On Tuesday, she swam 6 laps, and on Wednesday, she swam 9 laps. If the pattern continues, how many laps will Sasha swim on Friday?

_____ laps

2. If the pattern of numbers continues, what would the "Out" number be if 9 is put in the "In" column? (*Write your answer on the line.*)

In	0	1	2	3	4	5
Out	3	4	5	6	7	8

_____

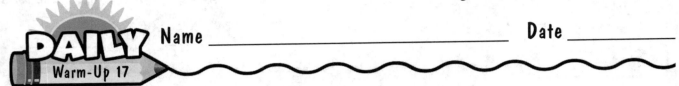

Warm-Up 17

1. Draw the next figure in the pattern.

2. Write the missing number in the box that will make each number sentence true.

A. 2 x 2 = 2 + ☐   **D.** 6 x 2 = 3 x ☐   **G.** 2 x 5 = 8 + ☐

B. 9 – ☐ = 2 x 4   **E.** 4 x ☐ = 2 x 8   **H.** 8 x ☐ = 2 x 4

C. 3 x 3 = 9 x ☐   **F.** 5 x 1 = 4 + ☐   **I.** 4 x 3 = 2 x ☐

- -

Warm-Up 18

1. The number in each circle is the sum of the numbers in the rectangles surrounding the circle. Can you find the missing numbers in the triangle puzzle?

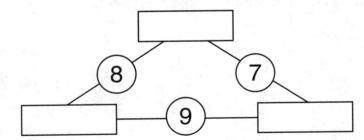

2. Look at each number. What is the pattern between the "In" and "Out" numbers? Complete the table and identify the rule.

In	0	1	2	3	4	5	**What is the rule?**
Out	0	4	8	12			

Name _____ **Date** _____

1. Which figure comes next in the pattern? (*Circle the correct letter.*)

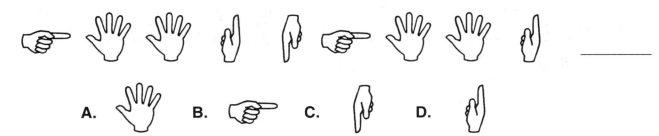

A. **B.** **C.** **D.**

2. Fill in the missing number that makes the problem true. (*Circle the correct letter.*)

$$6 \times 2 = 9 + \underline{\hspace{1cm}}$$

A. 2   **B.** 3   **C.** 4   **D.** 5

Name _____ **Date** _____

1. Fill in the missing number that makes the problem true.

$$21 + y = 3 \times 7$$

$$y = \underline{\hspace{1cm}}$$

2. What is happening to the "In" numbers to get the "Out" numbers?

In	2	4	6	8
Out	4	8	12	16

DAILY Warm-Up 21

Name _____ Date _____

1. Write the rule for each table below.

A.

In	2	3	4	5	6	7
Out	6	9	12	15	18	21

What is the rule? _____

_____

B.

In	0	1	2	3	4	5
Out	3	4	5	6	7	8

What is the rule? _____

_____

2. Write the missing number in the box that will make each number sentence true.

A. 5 + 2 = 3 + ☐

B. 3 + 2 = 4 + ☐

C. 7 + 7 = 4 + ☐

D. 4 + 4 = 2 + ☐

E. 5 + 3 = 1 + ☐

F. 1 + 6 = 3 + ☐

G. 5 + 3 = 5 + ☐

H. 4 + 7 = 8 + ☐

I. 3 + 4 = 5 + ☐

DAILY Warm-Up 22

Name _____ Date _____

1. What is the missing number in the pattern? (*Circle the correct letter.*)

A. 20

B. 21

C. 22

D. 23

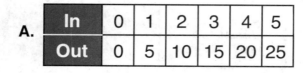

4, 10, 16, _____ , 28

2. Write the rule for each table below.

A.

In	0	1	2	3	4	5
Out	0	5	10	15	20	25

What is the rule? _____

_____

B.

In	2	3	4	5	6	7
Out	3	4	5	6	7	8

What is the rule? _____

_____

©Teacher Created Resources, Inc.

DAILY Warm-Up 23

Name _____ Date _____

1. What number is missing in the pattern below?

16, 21, 26, 31, 36, _____

2. Which pattern below is like the pattern in the box? (*Circle the correct letter.*)

| 1 | 1 | 1 | 2 | 3 | 1 | 1 | 1 | 2 | 3 |

A. 5 5 6 5 5 5 6 5 5 6

B. 4 9 4 9 4 9 4 9 4 9

C. 6 6 6 7 8 6 6 6 7 8

D. 5 5 5 6 7 8 9 5 5 5

DAILY Warm-Up 24

Name _____ Date _____

1. Look at the table. Continuing the pattern, fill in the "Out" number if 8 is put in the "In" column.

In	Out
4	8
6	12
8	

2. Larry has a container of marbles. If he counted the marbles by 9s, which pattern shows how Larry would have counted? (*Circle the correct letter.*)

A. 9, 19, 27, 36   **C.** 9, 18, 29, 36

B. 9, 18, 27, 36   **D.** 9, 18, 27, 34

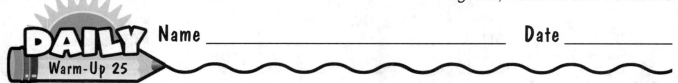

Name _____ **Date** _____

Warm-Up 25

1. On Monday, Laurie read 3 pages in her book. On Tuesday, she read 6 pages and on Wednesday she read 9 pages. Continue the pattern in the table below. How many pages will Laurie read on Saturday? (*Circle your final answer.*)

Day	Monday	Tuesday	Wednesday	Thursday	Friday	Saturday
Pages Read	3	6	9			

2. What shape comes next in the pattern? (*Circle the correct letter.*)

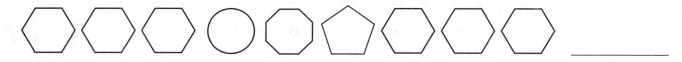

A. **B.** **C.** **D.**

Name _____ **Date** _____

Warm-Up 26

1. Jackie drew a pattern on the board for her best friend. She asked her friend to draw the missing shapes in the pattern. If her friend drew them correctly, which two shapes did she draw? (*Circle the correct letter.*)

A. **B.** **C.** **D.**

2. Write the missing number in the box that will make each number sentence true.

A. $11 + 5 = 2 \times \boxed{}$　　**C.** $4 + 12 = 8 \times \boxed{}$　　**E.** $2 \times 6 = 5 + \boxed{}$

B. $10 + 10 = 2 \times \boxed{}$　　**D.** $5 + 10 = 3 \times \boxed{}$　　**F.** $5 + 9 = 2 \times \boxed{}$

Name _____ **Date** _____

DAILY Warm-Up 27

1. The chart shows the number of glasses of water Leroy drank during one week. If the pattern continued, fill in the number of glasses Leroy drank on Saturday.

Number of Glasses Drank	
Sunday	2
Monday	6
Tuesday	9
Wednesday	13
Thursday	16
Friday	20
Saturday	

2. What is the missing number in the pattern?

A. 65

B. 80

C. 90

D. 95

75, 80, 85, _____ , 95, 100

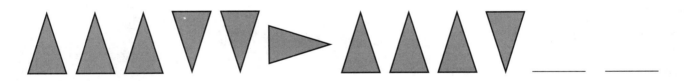

Name _____ **Date** _____

DAILY Warm-Up 28

1. Draw the next two figures in the pattern.

2. Write the missing number in the box that will make each number sentence true.

A. $6 \times 2 = 9 +$ ☐

B. $8 -$ ☐ $= 2 \times 4$

C. $3 + 2 = 5 \times$ ☐

D. $6 \times 2 = 3 \times$ ☐

E. $5 \times$ ☐ $= 2 \times 5$

F. $7 \times 1 = 3 +$ ☐

G. $2 \times 5 = 5 +$ ☐

H. $4 -$ ☐ $= 2 \times 2$

I. $4 \times 3 = 3 \times$ ☐

Name _____   **Date** _____

Warm-Up 29

1. The table shows the number of candies in different numbers of packages. Complete the table to find how many pieces of candy Bobby will have if he buys 3 packages of candy.

Number of Packages	Number of Candy
1	4
3	
5	20
7	28

2. Which number sentence is in the same fact family as 4 x 3 = 12? (*Circle the correct letter.*)

A. 12 ÷ 4 = 3   **B.** 4 + 3 = 7   **C.** 12 x 3 = 36   **D.** 12 x 4 = 48

Name _____   **Date** _____

Warm-Up 30

1. Tim has a box of marbles. If he takes the marbles out in groups of 3, which list shows how Tim would have counted? (*Circle the correct letter.*)

A. 3, 6, 9, 10

B. 3, 6, 8, 12

C. 6, 9, 12, 15

D. 3, 6, 9, 12

2. Look at the T-chart. Explain how the "IN" and "OUT" numbers are related.

_____

_____

_____

_____

IN	OUT
1	4
2	5
3	6
4	7
5	8

DAILY Warm-Up 31

Name _____ Date _____

1. Peggy plans to buy 2 pieces of candy for each trick-or-treater who comes to her door on Halloween. Which table below correctly shows how many pieces of candy she will need to buy if 4, 8, 10, or 12 trick-or-treaters show up on Halloween? (*Circle the correct letter.*)

A.

Trick-or-Treaters	Candy Needed
4	8
8	16
10	20
12	24

B.

Trick-or-Treaters	Candy Needed
4	6
8	10
10	12
12	14

C.

Trick-or-Treaters	Candy Needed
4	2
8	6
10	8
12	10

D.

Trick-or-Treaters	Candy Needed
4	8
8	11
10	16
12	10

2. Brandi is teaching an art project to her cousins. For each project she does, she needs 2 sheets of paper. The table shows the sheets of paper she will need for different numbers of projects. If Brandi does 6 projects with her cousins, how many sheets of paper will she need?

Number of Projects	1	2	3	4	5	6	7	8
Sheets of Paper	2	4	6	8	10		14	16

DAILY Warm-Up 32

Name _____ Date _____

1. The table shows the number of markers in different numbers of packages. After you find the rule, figure out how many markers are in 6 packages of markers?

_____ markers

Number of Packages	Number of Markers
1	5
3	15
5	25
7	35
8	40

2. Write four number sentences for the numbers 14, 7, and 2.

_____ X _____ = _____   _____ ÷ _____ = _____

_____ X _____ = _____   _____ ÷ _____ = _____

Name _____ **Date** _____

DAILY Warm-Up 33

1. What's happening to the numbers in the "In" column to get the numbers in the "Out" column?

In	10	9	8	7	6	5
Out	7	6	5	4	3	2

_____

_____

_____

2. Continue the pattern of numbers in the boxes below. What are the missing numbers?

3	5	7	9			13	15	

_____ and _____

- -

Name _____ **Date** _____

DAILY Warm-Up 34

1. It is the first day of school. Bobby is trying to find his class. He passed the following room numbers on his way. Which number would he most likely see on the next door? (*Circle the correct letter.*)

A. 225

B. 223

C. 227

D. 230

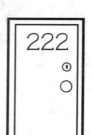

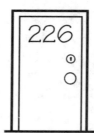

2. The table shows the color of hats Jeffrey has. Based on the pattern, how many blue hats does Jeffrey have?

Number	2	5	8	11	14	
Color	Yellow	Red	Purple	Green	Orange	Blue

DAILY Warm-Up 35

Name _____ Date _____

1. James is playing a number game with his son. Look at the table of numbers he has used. If James put in the number 6 in the "IN" side, what would be the number in the "OUT" side? Write this number on the table.

IN	OUT
14	7
12	6
10	5
8	4
6	

2. Write the missing number in the box that will make each number sentence true.

A. 2 x 3 = 4 + ☐

B. 5 x ☐ = 8 + 2

C. 4 x 2 = 10 – ☐

D. 2 x 2 = 4 + ☐

E. 1 x ☐ = 4 + 3

F. 8 x 2 = 4 x ☐

G. 5 x 3 = 7 + ☐

H. 6 x ☐ = 8 + 4

I. 7 x 2 = 14 – ☐

DAILY Warm-Up 36

Name _____ Date _____

1. Look at the pattern of circles. Which expression shows how to find the total number of circles? (*Circle the correct letter.*)

A. 8 – 2 = 6

B. 8 + 2 = 10

C. 8 x 2 = 16

D. 8 ÷ 2 = 4

○○○○○○○○
○○○○○○○

2. Complete the number sentences for the 4, 9, and 36 fact family. The first one is done for you.

9　x　4　=　36　　　　____ ÷ ____ = ____

____ x ____ = ____　　　　____ ÷ ____ = ____

DAILY
Warm-Up 37

Name _____ Date _____

1. Andrew has a stack of cards he wants to divide equally with his friends. If he counted the cards by 8s, which list shows how Andrew would have counted them? (*Circle the correct letter.*)

A. 8, 12, 18, 32   **C.** 8, 16, 24, 36

B. 8, 12, 16, 24   **D.** 8, 16, 24, 32

2. What number is missing in the pattern below?

16,   24,   32,   40,   48,   ☐

DAILY
Warm-Up 38

Name _____ Date _____

1. Write the missing number in the box that will make each number sentence true.

A. ☐ + 4 = 8 + 3   **D.** ☐ − 4 = 8 + 3   **G.** ☐ + 4 = 4 x 2

B. 7 + 3 = 1 + ☐   **E.** 7 − 3 = 1 + ☐   **H.** 7 + 3 = 1 x ☐

C. 2 + ☐ = 3 + 5   **F.** 2 + ☐ = 9 − 1   **I.** 2 x ☐ = 3 + 5

2. The table shows how many markers are in different numbers of packages. How many markers are in 10 packages? (*Circle the correct letter.*)

A. 38   **C.** 44

B. 40   **D.** 46

Number of Packages	Number of Markers
2	8
4	16
6	24
7	28
10	
12	48

Name _____ **Date** _____

1. If the rectangle represents "A", the circle represents "B", and the triangle represents "C", draw an AABCAABC pattern with the figures below.

____ ____ ____ ____ ____ ____ ____ ____

2. Look at the table. What is the pattern between the "In" and "Out" numbers? Complete the table and find the rule.

In	1	2	3	4	5	6	**What is the rule?**
Out	3	6	9	12			

Name _____ **Date** _____

1. The chart shows the number of pages Courtney read over five days. If the pattern continues, how many pages will Courtney read on Saturday? Write your answer in the table.

Number of Pages Read	
Monday	5
Tuesday	9
Wednesday	14
Thursday	18
Friday	23
Saturday	

2. What is the missing number in the pattern? (*Circle the correct letter.*)

A. 180

B. 190

C. 200

D. 210

120, 140, 160, ____ , 200, 220

Name _____ **Date** _____

Warm-Up 41

1. Complete the fact family for the numbers 2, 4, and 8.

_____ X _____ = _____   _____ ÷ _____ = _____

_____ X _____ = _____   _____ ÷ _____ = _____

2. Write the missing number in the box that will make each number sentence true.

A. 2 x 5 = 3 + ☐   **D.** 1 x 4 = 2 + ☐   **G.** 9 x 2 = 9 + ☐

B. 5 + 3 = 4 x ☐   **E.** 1 + 8 = 5 + ☐   **H.** 7 + 2 = 3 x ☐

C. 6 − 3 = 1 x ☐   **F.** 3 x 3 = 5 + ☐   **I.** 7 − 3 = 1 x ☐

Name _____ **Date** _____

Warm-Up 42

1. Liz needs 4 party favors for each child who comes to her niece's birthday party. Which table below correctly shows the number of party favors she will need if 4, 6, 8 or 10 children come to the party? (*Circle the correct letter.*)

A.

# of Children	Party Favors
4	16
6	24
8	12
10	40

B.

# of Children	Party Favors
4	16
6	10
8	32
10	40

C.

# of Children	Party Favors
4	16
6	24
8	32
10	40

D.

# of Children	Party Favors
4	8
6	10
8	12
10	14

2. Timothy has a jar of cubes he wants to share with his brothers and sisters. If he counted the cubes by 7s, which list shows how Timothy would have counted them? (*Circle the correct letter.*)

A. 7, 14, 21, 28   **C.** 7, 14, 23, 29

B. 7, 15, 21, 28   **D.** 7, 14, 22, 28

DAILY
Warm-Up 43

Name _____   **Date** _____

1. The table shows the number of beads Marissa needs for different numbers of bracelets. If the pattern continues, how many beads will she need to make 5 bracelets?

Number of Bracelets	Number of Beads
1	8
2	16
3	24
4	32

She will need _____ beads.

2. Write four number sentences for the numbers 3, 5, and 15.

_____ X _____ = _____   _____ ÷ _____ = _____

_____ X _____ = _____   _____ ÷ _____ = _____

- -

DAILY
Warm-Up 44

Name _____   **Date** _____

1. Matthew arranged the figures below in a pattern. What two shapes come next in the pattern? (*Circle the correct letter.*)

A. 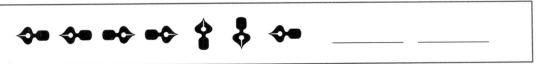   B.   C.   D.

2. Which number sentence is in the same fact family as 4 x 8 = 32? (*Circle the correct letter.*)

A. 8 − 4 = 4   **C.** 32 ÷ 4 = 8

B. 8 + 4 = 12   **D.** 32 − 4 = 28

1. Jacob went to the store to purchase sodas. The sodas came in packs of 6. Which could be the number of sodas Jacob bought? (*Circle the correct letter.*)

A. 25   **B.** 22

C. 20   **D.** 24

2. Fill in the missing number in the pattern below.

13, 22, 31, 40, 49, ☐

---

1. Gordon swam in his pool 2 laps on Monday, 4 laps on Tuesday, and 6 laps on Wednesday. If this pattern continues, how many laps will Gordon swim on Friday?

_____ laps

2. The table shows the number of tennis balls that are in different numbers of containers. How many tennis balls are in 4 containers? (*Circle the correct letter.*)

A. 16   **C.** 24

B. 20   **D.** 28

# of Containers	# of Tennis Balls
1	4
2	8
3	12
4	
5	20
6	24

Name _____   **Date** _____

DAILY
Warm-Up 47

1. Write four number sentences for the numbers 5, 8, and 40.

_____ ÷ _____ = _____   _____ X _____ = _____

_____ ÷ _____ = _____   _____ X _____ = _____

2. Look at the pattern of numbers. Which is **true** about the numbers?

    A. They will always be even.

    B. They will start with an even number.

    C. They will end with an even number.

    D. They will always be odd.

9, 13, 17, 21, _____

Name _____   **Date** _____

DAILY
Warm-Up 48

1. Place the numbers in the box below in the grid at the right to make 15 in each direction. Cross out each number once it has been used.

Number Choices
1 2 3 5 6

4		8
9		
	7	

2. If the pattern of numbers continues, what would be the "Out" number if 6 is put into the "In" column? (*Write your answer on the line.*)

In	0	1	2	3	4	5
Out	3	4	5	6	7	8

_____

Name _____ **Date** _____

1. Mr. Basil drew the pattern of math signs on the board. If the pattern continues, what would be the next two signs in the pattern? (*Circle the correct letter.*)

$$\div \ \div \ \times \ + \ - \ \div \ \div \ \times \ + \ - \ \_\_\_\_\_ \ \_\_\_\_\_$$

A. $\div \ \div$ **B.** $\times \ +$ **C.** $- \ \div$ **D.** $\div \ \times$

2. Which number sentence is in the same fact family as 5 x 9 = 45? (*Circle the correct letter.*)

A. $9 - 5 = 4$ **B.** $9 + 5 = 14$ **C.** $45 \div 5 = 9$ **D.** $40 - 5 = 35$

- -

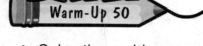

Name _____ **Date** _____

1. Solve the problems.

A. $(3 \times 2) \times 2 =$ _____   **B.** $(4 \times 3) \times 0 =$ _____

2. James wrote this pattern of numbers on the board. What comes next in the pattern?

$$500, \ 1{,}000, \ 1{,}500, \ \_\_\_\_\_$$

DAILY
Warm-Up 51

Name _____ Date _____

1. Draw the missing letter in the pattern below.

AABCAAB ___

2. Write the missing number in the box that will make each number sentence true.

A. 5 x 4 = 2 x ☐   **D.** 5 x 2 = 2 x ☐   **G.** 3 x 2 = 2 x ☐

B. 6 x 2 = 1 x ☐   **E.** 7 x 2 = 1 x ☐   **H.** 2 x 7 = 7 x ☐

C. 5 x 3 = 3 x ☐   **F.** 3 x 3 = 9 x ☐   **I.** 3 x 2 = 6 x ☐

- -

DAILY
Warm-Up 52

Name _____ Date _____

1. Look at the table below.

In	18	17	16	15	14	13
Out	9	8	7	6	5	4

What is being done to the "In" numbers to get the "Out" numbers?

_____

_____

2. On 1 hand, there are 5 fingers. On 2 hands, there are 10 fingers, and on 3 hands there are 15 fingers. Fill in the number of fingers there are on 10 hands.

Number of Hands	1	2	3	4	5	6	7	8	9	10
Number of Fingers	5	10	15	20	25	30	35	40	45	

DAILY Warm-Up 53   Name _____   Date _____

1. Linda wants to give 4 pieces of candy to each of her friends. Which table shows the total candy Linda will need for different numbers of friends? (*Circle the correct letter.*)

A.

# of Friends	Candy Needed
1	5
2	6
3	7
4	8

B.

# of Friends	Candy Needed
4	16
5	20
6	24
7	28

C.

# of Friends	Candy Needed
12	8
13	9
14	10
15	11

D.

# of Friends	Candy Needed
16	4
20	5
24	6
28	7

2. Look at the table. How many paintbrushes are in 8 packages?

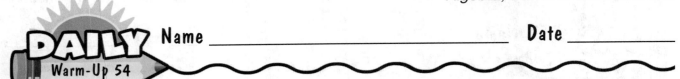

Number of Packages	1	2	3	4	5	6	7	8
Number of Paintbrushes	2	4	6	8	10	12	14	

There are _____ paintbrushes in 8 packages.

- -

DAILY Warm-Up 54   Name _____   Date _____

1. The table shows the number of crayons in different numbers of boxes. How many crayons are in 4 boxes?

Number of Boxes	Number of Crayons
1	5
3	15
4	
5	25
7	35
8	40

_____ crayons

2. Write four number sentences for the numbers 24, 6, and 4.

_____ X _____ = _____   _____ ÷ _____ = _____

_____ X _____ = _____   _____ ÷ _____ = _____

       ©Teacher Created Resources, Inc.

DAILY Warm-Up 55

Name _____ Date _____

1. What numbers come next in the pattern?

6, 6, 6, 7, 7, 8, 8, 8, 9, 9, 10, _____ , _____

2. What is being done to the "In" numbers to get the "Out" numbers?

In	14	13	12	11	10	9
Out	9	8	7	6	5	4

_____

_____

_____

DAILY Warm-Up 56

Name _____ Date _____

1. Fernando arranged paintbrushes in the pattern below. What operation best shows how he arranged them? (*Circle the correct letter.*)

A. 8 x 3

B. 3 x 9

C. 3 + 9

D. 3 + 8

2. The squares below increase in size. If the pattern continues, what will the length be on the next square?

5 cm   15 cm   25 cm   _____

DAILY Warm-Up 57

Name _____ Date _____

1. Fill in the number that is missing in the pattern.

53	47	41	35	29	

2. Circle *True* if the number in the box makes the statement correct or *False* if it does not.

A. $13 + \boxed{8} = 7 \times 3$ **TRUE or FALSE**

B. $8 \times \boxed{2} = 8 + 8$ **TRUE or FALSE**

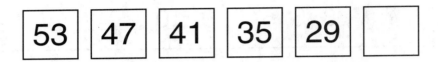

DAILY Warm-Up 58

Name _____ Date _____

1. One cow has 4 legs. How many legs do 5 cows have?

Number of Cows	Number of Legs
1	4
2	8
3	12
4	16
5	

_____ legs

2. Draw the missing shapes in the pattern.

        _____ _____

Name _____ **Date** _____

1. Draw the missing shape in the pattern below.

2. Write the missing number in the box that will make each number sentence true.

A. 4 x 4 = 2 x ☐   **D.** 4 x 3 = 2 x ☐   **G.** 2 x 9 = 18 x ☐

B. 3 x 3 = 9 x ☐   **E.** 2 x 6 = 3 x ☐   **H.** 2 x 7 = 7 x ☐

C. 6 x 1 = 2 x ☐   **F.** 7 x 3 = 3 x ☐   **I.** 4 x 6 = 3 x ☐

Name _____ **Date** _____

1. Look at the table below. What is being done to the "In" numbers to get the "Out" numbers?

In	17	16	15	14	13	12
Out	12	11	10	9	8	7

_____

_____

2. On 1 tricycle, there are 3 tires. On 2 tricycles, there are 6 tires and on 3 tricycles there are 9 tires. Fill in the number of tires there are on 10 tricycles.

Number of Tricycles	1	2	3	4	5	6	7	8	9	10
Number of Tires	3	6	9	12	15	18	21	24	27	

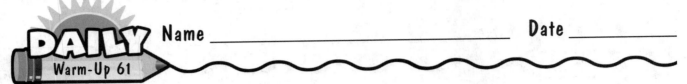

Name _____ **Date** _____

Warm-Up 61

1. Which card would be next in the pattern?

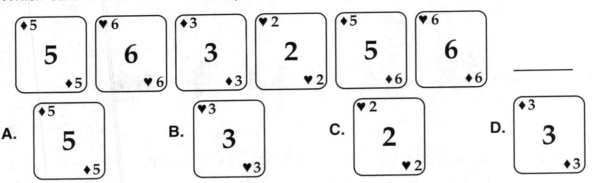

A. [card: ♦5 / 5 / ♦5]   B. [card: ♥3 / 3 / ♥3]   C. [card: ♥2 / 2 / ♥2]   D. [card: ♦3 / 3 / ♦3]

2. Which pattern is this?

A. ABABAB

B. AABCAABC

C. AABAAB

D. AABAABAA

- -

Name _____ **Date** _____

Warm-Up 62

1. Look at the pattern of numbers. Fill in the next two numbers.

$$60, 52, 44, 36, 28, \underline{\hspace{1cm}} , \underline{\hspace{1cm}}$$

How did you find the missing numbers?

_____

2. Write four number sentences for the numbers 21, 7, and 3.

_____ X _____ = _____   _____ ÷ _____ = _____

_____ X _____ = _____   _____ ÷ _____ = _____

Answer Key

Warm-Up 1
1. C   2. 47

Warm-Up 2
1. 10 miles   2. A

Warm-Up 3
1. C   2. 60

Warm-Up 4
1. 30
2. 2 x 6 = 12
   6 x 2 = 12
   12 ÷ 2 = 6
   12 ÷ 6 = 2

Warm-Up 5
1. 12   2. C

Warm-Up 6
1. C
2. 43; From left to right, the pattern is decreasing by 9.

Warm-Up 7
1. A   2. C

Warm-Up 8
1. B
2. Each "In" number is multiplied by 4 to produce the "Out" number.

Warm-Up 9
1. B   2. D

Warm-Up 10
1. D
2. Each "In" number is multiplied by 2 to produce the "Out" number.

Warm-Up 11
1. ♥
2. A. 8   D. 8   G. 3
   B. 10   E. 4   H. 2
   C. 5   F. 9   I. 1

Warm-Up 12
1. 5 is being subtracted
2. 20

Warm-Up 13
1. A. 9   D. 8   G. 18
   B. 8   E. 7   H. 1
   C. 2   F. 1   I. 4

2.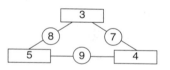

Warm-Up 14
1. 7, 8   2. 8 miles

Warm-Up 15
1. D   2. 48

Warm-Up 16
1. 15 laps   2. 12

Warm-Up 17
1. ▣

2. A. 2   D. 4   G. 2
   B. 1   E. 4   H. 1
   C. 1   F. 1   I. 6

Warm-Up 18
1.

2. 16, 20; Rule: Multiply the "In" number by 4 to get the "Out" number.

Warm-Up 19
1. C   2. B

Warm-Up 20
1. y = 0
2. The "In" number is being multiplied by 2 to get the "Out" number.

Warm-Up 21
1. A. Multiply the "In" number by 3 to get the "Out" number.
   B. Add 3 to the "In" number to get the "Out" number.

2. A. 4   D. 6   G. 3
   B. 1   E. 7   H. 3
   C. 10   F. 4   I. 2

Warm-Up 22
1. C
2. A. Multiply the "In" number by 5 to get the "Out" number.
   B. Add 1 to the "In" number to get the "Out" number.

Warm-Up 23
1. 41   2. C

Warm-Up 24
1. 16   2. B

Warm-Up 25
1. 12, 15, ⑱   2. D

Warm-Up 26
1. B
2. A. 8   D. 5
   B. 10   E. 7
   C. 2   F. 7

Warm-Up 27
1. 23   2. C

Warm-Up 28
1.

2. A. 3   D. 4   G. 5
   B. 0   E. 2   H. 0
   C. 1   F. 4   I. 4

Warm-Up 29
1. 12   2. A

Warm-Up 30
1. D
2. Add 3 to each "In" number to get the "Out" number.

Warm-Up 31
1. A   2. 12

Answer Key

Warm-Up 32
1. 30 markers
2. 2 x 7 = 14
   7 x 2 = 14
   14 ÷ 2 = 7
   14 ÷ 7 = 2

Warm-Up 33
1. Subtract 3 from the "In" number to get the "Out" number.
2. 11 and 17

Warm-Up 34
1. D   2. 17

Warm-Up 35
1. 3
2. A. 2   D. 0   G. 8
   B. 2   E. 7   H. 2
   C. 2   F. 4   I. 0

Warm-Up 36
1. C
2. 4 x 9 = 36
   36 ÷ 4 = 9
   36 ÷ 9 = 4

Warm-Up 37
1. D   2. 56

Warm-Up 38
1. A. 7   D. 15   G. 4
   B. 9   E. 3   H. 10
   C. 6   F. 6   I. 4
2. B

Warm-Up 39
1. □□○△□□○△
2. 15, 18; Rule: Multiply the "In" number by 3 to get the "Out" number.

Warm-Up 40
1. 27   2. A

Warm-Up 41
1. 2 x 4 = 8
   4 x 2 = 8
   8 ÷ 4 = 2
   8 ÷ 2 = 4

2. A. 7   D. 2   G. 9
   B. 2   E. 4   H. 3
   C. 3   F. 4   I. 4

Warm-Up 42
1. C   2. A

Warm-Up 43
1. 40 beads
2. 3 x 5 = 15
   5 x 3 = 15
   15 ÷ 3 = 5
   15 ÷ 5 = 3

Warm-Up 44
1. C   2. C

Warm-Up 45
1. D   2. 58

Warm-Up 46
1. 10 laps   2. A

Warm-Up 47
1. 40 ÷ 5 = 8
   40 ÷ 8 = 5
   5 x 8 = 40
   8 x 5 = 40
2. D

Warm-Up 48
1.

4	3	8
9	5	1
2	7	6

2. The "Out" number will be 9.

Warm-Up 49
1. A   2. C

Warm-Up 50
1. A. 12   2. 2,000
   B. 0

Warm-Up 51
1. C
2. A. 10   D. 5   G. 3
   B. 12   E. 14   H. 2
   C. 5   F. 1   I. 1

Warm-Up 52
1. 9 is being subtracted from the "In" number to get the "Out" number.
2. 50

Warm-Up 53
1. B   2. 16

Warm-Up 54
1. 20 crayons
2. 4 x 6 = 24
   6 x 4 = 24
   24 ÷ 4 = 6
   24 ÷ 6 = 4

Warm-Up 55
1. 10, 10
2. 5 is being subtracted from the "In" number to get the "Out" number.

Warm-Up 56
1. B   2. 35 cm

Warm-Up 57
1. 23
2. A. True   B. True

Warm-Up 58
1. 20 legs   2. ♡ ♡

Warm-Up 59
1. ◆
2. A. 8   D. 6   G. 1
   B. 1   E. 4   H. 2
   C. 3   F. 7   I. 8

Warm-Up 60
1. 5 is being subtracted from the "In" number to get the "Out" number.
2. 30

Warm-Up 61
1. D   2. D

Warm-Up 62
1. 20, 12; Subtract 8 from the previous number.
2. 7 x 3 = 21
   3 x 7 = 21
   21 ÷ 7 = 3
   21 ÷ 3 = 7